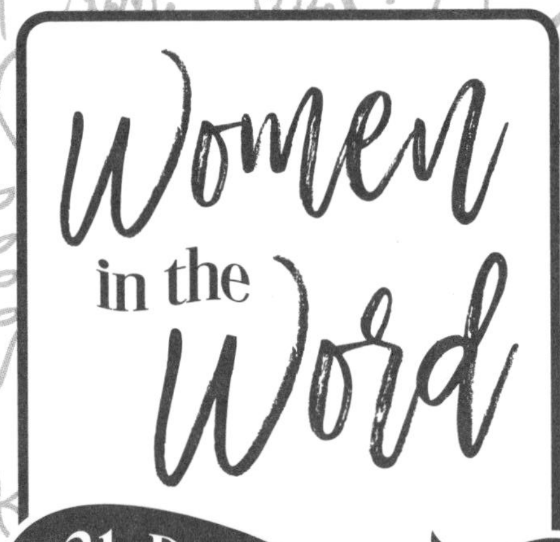

A 31-Day Devotional

AMAZING FACTS

Women in the Word: A 31-Day Devotional

Printed in the U.S.A.

Published by Amazing Facts, Inc.
P.O. Box 1058
Roseville, CA 95678
916-434-3880
afbookstore.com

Content editing by Laurie Lyon
Cover and text design by Haley Trimmer
Text layout by Greg Solie • Altamont Graphics

ISBN: 978-1-58019-597-3

Introduction

Bonnie Ensminger
Executive Assistant to Pastor Doug Batchelor

Many years ago, Pastor Glenn Coon, a dynamic preacher, came to my town and shared a poem by Mildred Hill that I have never forgotten:

> Lord, make me a nail upon the wall,
> fastened securely in its place.
> Then from this thing so common and so small,
> hang a bright picture of Thy face.

From that day forward, this poem has been my prayer and heart's desire.

I wish I could say that I have always been this kind of a person. As a young wife and mother of three children in just four years, it was a very busy life. I had two babies in diapers and another one running around—this being before the days of disposables.

But keeping a positive attitude and believing the promises of God has been a blessing to me through the years of babies, children, teenagers, college students, young adults, adults, grandchildren, sickness, sorrows, and death.

In times of despair, I have found myself clinging to the promise of John 14:1–3:

> Let not your heart be troubled; you believe in God, believe also in Me. In My Father's house are many mansions; if it were not so, I would have told you. I go to prepare a place for you. And if I go and prepare a place for you, I will come again and receive you to Myself; that where I am, there you may be also.

"Let" means to allow or permit. Then "Let not" means not to allow something. So don't allow your heart to be troubled! We have a choice. There's so much trouble all about us: war and terrorist attacks, crime and violence, and economic pressures. Your worries and fears may be intensely personal. Whatever they are, choose not to let your heart be troubled, because we believe in God, and He has prepared a place for us!

So today, choose to focus on the promises of God in your life. Be intentional about starting each day in His Word—maybe even starting with this devotional, written by the women of Amazing Facts or the wives and sisters of staff—considering the ways in which He has led the women of old.

And as we spend time dwelling on His promises, we too can find peace and comfort, regardless of the trial, knowing that He loves us and will soon take us to our eternal home.

Enjoy!

Day 1

Choosing to Choose

Karen Batchelor

> *"The rib which the LORD God had taken from man He made into a woman, and He brought her to the man." —Genesis 2:22*

Have you ever wondered how many choices a person makes in a day?

It is estimated that in sixteen hours, adults make an average of 23,328 choices. We make the majority of these instinctually, with little to no consideration of outcome. Other choices require us to think and decide based on facts, emotions, and needs.

Where does God fit into this picture of choice? Does He control each of our thoughts and actions? If so, do we really have the ability to choose? I believe God created us in His image and has given us the actual ability to make choices that will lead to eternal life or eternal death.

Choice is defined as: "1) An act or instance of choosing: selection. 2) The right, power, or opportunity to choose; option. 3) The person or thing chosen or eligible to be chosen" (Dictionary.com).

I see Eve in this definition.

Eve was the first "Whoa man!" ever created! God created her in His own image, and she was the first woman to experience living in the Garden of Eden, where everything was "good" and "very good." Everything was perfect—the weather, the animals, her home, the food she ate, and her husband!

Eve had the privilege of talking with God and His angels. The angels shared their first-hand experiences of a perfect heaven until pride and selfishness entered the heart of Satan and war broke out in heaven (Revelation 12:7–9). Satan used his cunning deceptions to deceive a third of the angels. "It was by disobedience to the just commands of God that Satan and his host had fallen."

The pair were encouraged to "be on their guard against the devices of Satan, for his efforts to ensnare them would be unwearied. While they were obedient to God, the evil one uld not harm them; for, if need be, every angel in heaven would be sent to their help. If they eadfastly repelled his first insinuations, they would be as secure as the heavenly messengers. ıt should they once yield to temptation, their nature would become so depraved that in emselves they would have no power and no disposition to resist Satan.

"God's love for us is so complete and freely given that we cannot fathom it! He wants know that we choose Him as He has chosen us. For that reason, He placed the tree of the owledge of good and evil at the center of the Garden as "a test of their obedience and their ve to God" (*Patriarchs and Prophets,* pp. 52, 53).

Eve became so absorbed in her work that she mindlessly wandered from her husband's de. Finding herself standing before the forbidden tree, she quieted her fears by telling herself at since God had warned her, she could spot evil and handle it. Curiously gazing at the tree d the serpent, she wondered why God would keep such beauty away from her. Through the rpent, Satan boosted her doubt in God and confidence in herself by saying, "You will not rely die. For God knows that in the day you eat of it your eyes will be opened, and you will be ke God, knowing good and evil" (Genesis 3:4, 5).

Are you seeing the choices Eve had already made in her day? The first few seemed nocent enough—but were they? Relying on her own wisdom, she decided that she would st *look* at the temptation. As the definition of choice says, she made the selection to be on er own. And, being eligible to be chosen, she was enticed by Satan. You and I know all too ell the result of her choices—sin was ushered into our world. We are all affected by Eve's nall choices.

Here are some biblical steps to making wiser choices in our daily lives, taken from the mazing Facts booklet *Determining the Will of God:*

- When we are willing and surrendered to God (John 7:17) . . .
- He will guide us by the law contained in His Word (Psalm 119:105).
- He will open doors for us (2 Corinthians 2:12) . . .
- As we pray (Psalm 55:16, 17) . . .
- Fast (Matthew 17:14–21) . . .
- Unselfishly seek God's kingdom (Matthew 6:33, 34) . . .
- And glorify God in all we do (1 Corinthians 10:31).
- We are guided by the Holy Spirit (Isaiah 30:21) . . .
- To be patient (2 Thessalonians 3:5) and faithful (Revelation 17:14) . . .
- Because God is faithful (1 Thessalonians 5:23, 24).

- God will then grant our heart's choice for Him (Psalm 20:4).
- We must look at the evidence (2 Corinthians 13:1) God gives for making our choices.
- Then God can use our choices to transform us (Romans 12:2).

I am amazed when I stop and realize that God loves me so much that He allows me to choose to follow Him or to turn away from Him. As a parent, I sometimes want to intervene in my adult children's lives, to help them make what I consider to be the best choice for them. B God doesn't do that. He honors my choices, even when they hurt Him and make the sacrifice of Christ irrelevant in my life. What a great and loving God! I want to make choices that will grow my relationship with Him. I choose Christ! I am praying that you will choose Him too! Will you join me?

"The Lord did not set His love on you nor choose you because you were more in number than any other people, for you were the least of all peoples; but because the Lord loves you" (Deuteronomy 7:7, 8).

"Fear the Lord, serve Him in sincerity and in truth, and put away the gods which your fathers served on the other side of the River and in Egypt. Serve the Lord! . . . Choose for yourselves this day whom you will serve" (Joshua 24:14, 15).

"Trust in the Lord with all your heart, and lean not on your own understanding; in all your ways acknowledge Him, and He shall direct your paths" (Proverbs 3:5, 6).

:ssons I Learned:

eflect on opportunities for self-improvement.)

:rsonal Goal for Today:

lentify one goal based on the reading.)

oday's Targets:

ist three practical steps to help you reach your goal.)

oday I am thankful for:

Write a short prayer of thanks to God for the blessings He has brought to you.)

Day 2

A Change of Identity

Carissa McSherry

"[God] gives life to the dead and calls those things which do not exist as though they did." —*Romans 4:17*

Have you ever wished that you could change your name? Or even your identity?

Her face turned bright red with embarrassment. With flushed cheeks and a racing heart, sh stammered, "I didn't laugh! It wasn't me!" But try as she might, the look on her face left her audience unconvinced.

"Oh, but you did," came the gentle reply from a Stranger and His two friends.

Sarah hung her head in shame. She really did want to believe it was all true. She longed to have the child she had always wanted! But how could she?

Since childhood, Sarah had eagerly looked forward to the day when she would be a mothe Every little girl dreamt of having children of her own someday, an inheritance that would make her husband proud. Those who could not bear children were seen as having been cursed by God and were even unwanted by their husbands. Surely that legacy wouldn't be hers! Or so she hope

The years of pain trudged on. Every time she heard the cries of a servant's child, her hea yearned to embrace that precious baby as her own. She longed to make her husband proud and to fulfill his heart's desire, but she couldn't. It seemed the gossiping tongues of others confirmed what she felt in her heart: She was a failure.

Twenty-five years earlier, Abraham had excitedly shared with her a message he had received from the Lord: "Get out of your country, from your family and from your father's hous to a land that I will show you. I will make you a great nation; I will bless you and make your name great" (Genesis 12:1, 2). Fears about the perilous journey into the unknown or frustratio about the challenges of tent dwelling didn't even come to her mind. One thought stood out to her: "I will make you a great nation." Sarah's heart leapt within her as she pondered the question, *Does that mean I still have the hope of being a mother?*

Throughout the years, this promise was repeatedly shared with Abraham, reinforcing his ith. But Sarah's own heart eventually grew cold, even to the point of offering Hagar to her isband in her stead. But throughout her pain and sin, Sarah was not forgotten. God knew e desires of her heart, and He planned on fulfilling her longing in a way far greater than she uld have ever imagined.

Now God reassured Abraham of His promise with Sarah specifically in mind: "As for Sarai ur wife, you shall not call her name Sarai, but Sarah shall be her name. And I will bless her d also give you a son by her" (Genesis 17:15, 16). After all these years, even faithful Abraham ubted God's Word, but regardless of their feelings, the Word of God would not fail them.

This name change, from Sarai to Sarah, signified that Sarah would "be a mother of tions; kings of peoples shall be from her" (verse 16). It also revealed a change in Sarah's rspective. No longer was her focus solely about having a child; she began to recognize the omise that the Messiah would come through her lineage!

By giving Sarah a new name, the Lord was reassuring her of a new identity. Though it emed impossible to mortal humans that an elderly woman could bear a child, the promise ould nonetheless be fulfilled—because God was the One who had made the promise!

Sarah still doubted her new identity at times. But regardless of her doubt, God never ave up on her—and He will never give up on you! Hebrews 11:11 paints a beautiful picture f how God remembered this matriarch of old: "By faith Sarah herself also received strength conceive seed, and she bore a child when she was past the age, because she judged Him ithful who had promised."

Our patient God recalled not her doubt nor her sins, but her faith! Before she even ecame a mother of nations, God could call her such because in Him the greatest of promises ould be fulfilled!

This is also true in our lives today. God sees things that are not as though they are, ecause in Him, without a doubt, they indeed *will be*.

A story recorded in a BBC article highlighted the lives of children living in rural Zambia.[1] hese children are known for their rather unusual names. One little boy, laboring hard under a eavy load, has the name Mulangani, which means "punish me" or "he who must be punished." thers include "bad luck," "I will be eaten," or even "kill him."

Amazingly, the village leaders are the ones who often give these horrifying names to hese innocent little ones to signify the circumstances of their birth—or sometimes it is imply a curse that the village leaders wish to place upon them. Imagine living day to day with his legacy imprinted upon you!

However, something incredible happens to these children if they later decide to becom Christians: They get a new name! Instead of being known as a failure or as a worthless individual, these new Christian believers can now choose a new identity! While some choose common biblical names—such as John or Mary—Mulangani, on the other hand, has a very special name in mind: Emanuel. He will tell you with a smile, "It means God is with me."

So also, God has promised to give us a new name! (See Revelation 2:17.) Maybe thus fa in your life, you've only known the name Failure, Shame, or Not Enough. Or maybe the years have seemed to pass you by like Sarah; you've doubted your new identity in Him, or you've wandered through the deserts of life questioning your purpose. But as in the lessons learned from Sarah, God promises to give you a new name, a brand-new identity in Him today! That promise, without a doubt, will be fulfilled. Second Corinthians 5:17 promises us, "If anyone is Christ, he is a new creation; old things have passed away; behold, all things have become new Today, this new identity can be your reality.

Would you like to experience the joy of living this new life in Jesus today?

Conversation

"I know the thoughts that I think toward you, says the Lord, thoughts of peace and not of evil, to give you a future and a hope. Then you will call upon Me and go and pray to Me, and I will listen to you. And you will seek Me and find Me, when you search for Me with all your heart" (Jeremiah 29:11–13).

"'My thoughts are not your thoughts, nor are your ways My ways,' says the Lord. 'For as the heavens are higher than the earth, so are My ways higher than your ways, and My thoughts than your thoughts'" (Isaiah 55:8, 9).

"[Be] confident of this very thing, that He who has begun a good work in you will complete it until the day of Jesus Christ" (Philippians 1:6).

---

1 http://www.bbc.com/news/magazine-39351167

Daily Reflection

essons I Learned:

'eflect on opportunities for self-improvement.)

ersonal Goal for Today:

'dentify one goal based on the reading.)

oday's Targets:

.

.

.

List three practical steps to help you reach your goal.)

Today I am thankful for:

(Write a short prayer of thanks to God for the blessings He has brought to you.)

Simple Faith

Rosemary McKenzie

*"I will instruct you and teach you in the way you should go;
I will guide you with My eye." —Psalm 32:8*

Can I trust God when circumstances seem uncertain and even contradictory?

As she heard the story of his prayer and the part she acted in answering it, she was convinced that God was inviting her to take a journey of faith. She was presented with th amazing opportunity to be a part of the lineage of the promised Savior of the world.

Rebekah had grown up in a home that cherished a knowledge of the true God. When she was abruptly faced with the life-changing proposal of marriage, she chose to trust in the providences of God. Her simple statement of faith was, "I will go" (Genesis 24:58).

Twenty years later, in answer to her and Isaac's fervent prayers, Rebekah became pregnant with twins. The pregnancy was difficult and she sought the Lord in her time of distress. "The Lord said to her: 'Two nations are in your womb, two peoples shall be separated from your body; one people shall be stronger than the other, and the older shall serve the younger'" (Genesis 25:23).

As her children grew, Rebekah studied their characteristics. She felt sure that the special blessings of the birthright rightly belonged to her younger son, Jacob. She remembered clearly the Word of the Lord to her before their birth. However, her husband Isaac did not share her conviction. He was attracted to the bold Esau and determined to give him the birthright blessing traditionally given to the oldest son.

Rebekah overheard Isaac's plans to secretly give the blessings of the birthright and spiritual heritage to Esau, in spite of God's promise to Jacob. She felt that the circumstances required her intervention—even though her strategy was in direct opposition to the principles of God's Law. "God had declared that Jacob should receive the birthright, and His word would have been fulfilled in His own time had they waited in faith for Him to work for em. But like many who now profess to be children of God, they were unwilling to leave the atter in His hands" (*Patriarchs and Prophets*, p. 180).

The aftermath of this episode resulted in Jacob fleeing from his home as a fugitive and veling to his uncle's home, where he was defrauded and treated with constant suspicion. e consequences to Rebekah included years of bitter repentance and separation from her loved son.

Rebekah did not live to see the fulfillment of God's promises in her son's life. Even ough the outcome of her choice resulted in tragedy, loss, and disappointment, God was not terred from His purposes. Amid the pain and sorrow, God was still working out His gracious ovidences and bringing about His plan of salvation—in His own time.

Like many other women of faith—including Sarah, Rachel, and Esther—Rebekah failed a critical moment to trust that God would take the responsibility to fulfill the promises in s Word in His own way. And yet, despite Rebekah's failure, God still worked—taking the ess that resulted to bring about His purposes. Romans 8:28 says, "We know that all things ork together for good to those who love God, to those who are the called according to His rpose." Often, we think that "all things" are the good things, or the right choices that we ake, but the text clearly says that God is able to make "all things"—including our mistakes, ır failures, and the missteps of others—to work together for the ultimate good. That is the iracle of His grace.

Jesus identifies His church as a pure woman (Revelation 12:1) that He is preparing His bride. He is constantly working "that He might sanctify and cleanse her with the ashing of water by the word, that He might present her to Himself a glorious church, t having spot or wrinkle or any such thing, but that she should be holy and without emish" (Ephesians 5:26, 27). Christ is in the business of taking our messy lives and turning em into beautiful examples of the miracle of His love.

In these last days of earth's history, God is calling His people to live lives of integrity with mplete faith in Him and His Word. Revelation declares, "Here is the patience of the saints; ere are those who keep the commandments of God and the faith of Jesus" (Revelation 14:12). e patience or endurance of the saints is manifest by their faithful lives of integrity, their eping of God's commandments through the grace of Christ, and their complete trust in Him accomplish their salvation through the power of His Word.

Today, when we are faced with the temptation to manipulate circumstances to meet our wn purposes, or even God's purposes, we can remember the lessons from the life of Rebekah. 'e can make a different choice—to trust God's timing rather than our own.

Christ's invitation to you today is to "Trust in the LORD with all your heart, and lean not o your own understanding; in all your ways acknowledge Him, and He shall direct your paths. D not be wise in your own eyes; fear the LORD and depart from evil. It will be health to your flesh and strength to your bones" (Proverbs 3:5–8).

"As for God, His way is perfect; the word of the LORD is proven; He is a shield to all who trust in Him" (2 Samuel 22:31).

"Trust in the LORD, and do good; dwell in the land, and feed on His faithfulness. Delight yourse also in the LORD, and He shall give you the desires of your heart. Commit your way to the LORD, trust also in Him, and He shall bring it to pass" (Psalm 37:3-5).

"Behold, God is my salvation, I will trust and not be afraid; 'For Yah, the LORD, is my strength ar song; He also has become my salvation.' Therefore with joy you will draw water from the wells of salvation." (Isaiah 12:2, 3).

Daily Reflection

essons I Learned:

___

___

___

___

eflect on opportunities for self-improvement.)

ersonal Goal for Today:

___

___

___

dentify one goal based on the reading.)

oday's Targets:

. ___

2. ___

3. ___

(List three practical steps to help you reach your goal.)

Today I am thankful for:

___

___

___

___

(Write a short prayer of thanks to God for the blessings He has brought to you.)

Serving One Another

Michelle Haas

"Well done, good and faithful servant; you were faithful over a few things, I will make you ruler over many things. Enter into the joy of your lord." —Matthew 25:21

Will a life of service end as a life of obscurity? How will you be remembered?

Parenting, or even babysitting, is most certainly an under-appreciated job. Cleaning the house can make you feel like you're a painter of the Golden Gate Bridge; after they finish painting from one end to the other, they start all over again! When you've finally cleaned the kitchen from breakfast, it's time for lunch . . . not to mention the list of things that still need to be done. And how will you be thanked for all of your hard work?

Did someone say 'thanked'?

Deborah probably felt this way quite often. As a handmaid, she was little more than a servant, which meant she would always live life in the servant caste. Perhaps she imagined being whisked away by some Prince Charming—or finding riches alongside the road that would change her life. But these things never came to pass; yet, she thrived! Deborah found peace in her existence and enjoyed her work. She was loved by the family she served, and her life provides a lesson for us, even today.

Rebekah was the daughter of Nahor and lived in the land of Mesopotamia. Genesis chapter 24 tells the story of how Rebekah came to marry Abraham's son Isaac, leaving her family home to travel to Canaan with Deborah. Did Deborah have a choice? Likely not. Which meant she was also leaving her home and traveling to a distant land with an unknown future. With such anonymity—she is not even mentioned by name when they departed Mesopotamia—it may be surprising that we read about her today.

Sir Isaac Newton's third law of motion states, "When one body exerts a force on a second body, the second body simultaneously exerts a force equal in magnitude and opposite in direction on the first body." We commonly say it as, "For every action there is an equal and opposite reaction." Serving others can often be a thankless job. As much as we are willing to give, there are always other people who are willing to take. Unfortunately, this often means that we take the path of least resistance—it's much easier to do nothing than to serve others.

Thankfully, we live much differently today than in Deborah's time. Our feet stay clean when we travel from city to city. New homes are almost guaranteed to have automatic dishwashers. Most of us have clean drinking water that pours from our faucets. Our lawn sprinklers are on automatic timers. Our garage doors raise and lower with the push of a button. We don't even have to get our hands wet to do our laundry. Yet somehow, with all of these advances, we seem to have *less* time to do what really matters! "Where do I possibly have time to volunteer?"

When we seek to help others, the blessing actually goes both ways. Have you ever helped someone in need? How did it make you feel afterward? In Luke 10:30–37, we find Jesus' parable of a man who fell among thieves. These vile predators stole from him, beat him until he was half dead, and left him lying in the road. A priest saw the man—and continued along his path. A Levite also saw the man, but crossed the street so that he didn't have to get close to the injured man's body.

Finally, a Samaritan came by and helped the victim, going above and beyond by putting the man up in a hotel for the night.

Leviticus 19:18 says, "You shall not take vengeance, nor bear any grudge against the children of your people, but you shall love your neighbor as yourself: I am the LORD." Jesus calls the Samaritan man in the story a "neighbor," someone who loved the injured man as himself (Luke 10:27, 36). Jesus was helping the people to understand that serving others joyfully is a big part of how we are to inherit eternal life.

There is a reason why Deborah has her place firmly etched into our shared history: She served with purpose! Genesis 35:8 says, "Deborah, Rebekah's nurse, died, and she was buried below Bethel under the terebinth tree. So the name of it was called Allon Bachuth."

In *Patriarchs and Prophets*, we find additional insight into Deborah's life of service:

> At Bethel, Jacob was called to mourn the loss of one who had long been an honored member of his father's family—Rebekah's nurse, Deborah, who had accompanied her mistress from Mesopotamia to the land of Canaan. The presence of this aged woman had been to Jacob a precious tie that bound him to his early life, and especially to the mother whose love for him had been so strong and tender. Deborah was buried

> with expressions of so great sorrow that the oak under which her grave was made, was called 'the oak of weeping.' It should not be passed unnoticed that the memory of her life of faithful service and of the mourning over this household friend has been accounted worthy to be preserved in the word of God (p. 206).

The story of Deborah teaches us that a life of service doesn't have to be a life of dread. We are appreciated when we are faithful servants—even if we are not always showered with appreciation. We are each blessed with a fragile life and make our choices each day as to how we will live our precious hours. Serving with distinction isn't just recognized by the people we know; it is recognized in the courts of heaven! By combining the lessons of Deborah's life with the words of Jesus, we get the big-picture understanding that we can and should serve others—not just for their blessing, but for *ours* too.

Conversation

"Whoever desires to become great among you, let him be your servant. And whoever desires to be first among you, let him be your slave—just as the Son of Man did not come to be served, but to serve, and to give His life a ransom for many" (Matthew 20:26–28).

"Do not use liberty as an opportunity for the flesh, but through love serve one another" (Galatians 5:13).

"As each one has received a gift, minister it to one another, as good stewards of the manifold grace of God" (1 Peter 4:10).

Lessons I Learned:

____

____

____

____

(Reflect on opportunities for self-improvement.)

Personal Goal for Today:

____

____

____

(Identify one goal based on the reading.)

Today's Targets:

1. ______________________________
2. ______________________________
3. ______________________________

(List three practical steps to help you reach your goal.)

Today I am thankful for:

____

____

____

____

(Write a short prayer of thanks to God for the blessings He has brought to you.)

Day 5

Critical Assignment

Laurie Lyon

"These words which I command you today shall be in your heart. You shall teach them diligently to your children." —Deuteronomy 6:6, 7

Have you ever felt inadequate in your ability to influence others spiritually?

Alice Mukarurinda clutched her nine-month-old baby with one hand and her nine-year-old niece with the other—and ran for her life as a bomb exploded into flames in the Rwandan church where she had been hiding. She ended up in a swamp, where she hid for days with only her face sticking out from the mud. But eventually the Hutus found her.

Emmanuel Ndayisaba, after killing her child and young niece, turned his machete on Alice. He sliced off her hand, cut a huge gash in her forehead, and left her for dead. Three days later, other survivors found Alice and helped her, and she gradually recovered.

A couple of years later, Emmanuel—a former choir member at a Christian church—could tolerate his nightmares no longer. Overcome with guilt, he turned himself in, confessing his crimes. Those participants who confessed their guilt were pardoned six years later.

Amazingly, Emmanuel knelt before Alice to ask for her forgiveness. After two weeks of soul searching, she forgave him because of what the Bible teaches—and the two have become friends. Alice and Emmanuel now work together with an organization that builds simple homes for genocide survivors. Emmanuel still wonders how he could have believed the foolish words and outright lies that caused him to perform such horrific acts.[2]

What lies were told about the Hebrew slaves that could have caused the Egyptian people to throw the helpless baby boys of the Israelites into the river to drown? The pharaoh's cruel order was in full effect when Jochebed bore her third child.

The Bible says that this Hebrew slave woman from the tribe of Levi did all she could to save her baby's life. First, she bravely hid him at home for three months. But, eventually, the risk became too great. So she carefully wove a small covered boat out of the bulrushes that grew at the water's edge. She waterproofed it, tucked her precious boy inside, and set it afloat on the crocodile-infested river. All the while, she prayed.

And God honored her prayer. When the daughter of the pharaoh came to the river to bathe, she spied the tiny watercraft and was intrigued. "When she opened it, she saw the child, and behold, the baby wept. So she had compassion on him" (Exodus 2:6). Indeed, she was so charmed by this beautiful child that she decided to adopt him.

Miriam, the baby's sister, came forward and asked if Pharaoh's daughter would like her to find a nurse for the baby. The princess, possibly reading between the lines, agreed. So Jochebed became the official caretaker of her own child for the next twelve years.

With a rock-solid faith in God and her belief that a deliverer had been promised to her people, she raised her son painstakingly in the ways of the Lord. Although she was a poor slave woman with an incredibly challenging life, the world has been tremendously blessed through her work with her son Moses.

Jochebed knew that soon her son would be swallowed up in a completely different environment—one that could lure him away from God. So she did everything she could to instill loyalty to God within the boy's heart. And it worked. "Those principles of truth that were the burden of his mother's teaching and the lesson of her life, no after influence could induce Moses to renounce" (*Reflecting Christ*, p. 327). In other words, what she taught him stuck like glue.

Even after attending the finest schools and military training that Egypt had to offer and learning the details of Egyptian religion, Moses clung to his belief in the true Creator and refused to worship heathen idols. As a great military leader, he came to be adored by the Egyptians. In the end, though, Moses chose to honor God and deliver His people from oppression, even though it meant forsaking the pleasures and honors of Egypt.

Jochebed took the responsibility of training her children very seriously. She was on an urgent mission, just like Eunice and Lois in the New Testament—mother and grandmother to Timothy. These devout Christian women carefully taught Timothy the Scriptures and how to apply them to his life in practical ways.

In a letter of encouragement to the young Timothy, the apostle Paul wrote that he was filled with joy when he remembered "the genuine faith that is in you, which dwelt first in your grandmother Lois and your mother Eunice, and I am persuaded is in you also" (2 Timothy 1:5). Because of what he learned from his devoted mother and grandmother, Timothy became a steadfast evangelist of the early Christian church, encouraging its members and building up disciples for the Lord.

Some people underestimate the importance of what a mother teaches her children, but nothing is more critical to the future of her offspring. By taking them out in nature and teaching them devotion to the Creator, and by sharing with them the rich treasures of God's Word, she shapes not only their future but also the future of every person they influence throughout their lives. Through this ripple effect, a mother's influence has an enormously wide range.

You may wonder, *Where do I get the wisdom and the strength for this critical assignment?* One thing is for certain, mothers can't do it alone! Our world is out of control and packed with temptations and distractions on every side. Only God can empower you to raise up your children to honor Him despite the evil around them. Only He can provide the wisdom mothers need.

In Paul's second letter to Timothy, he noted "that from childhood you have known the Holy Scriptures, which are able to make you wise for salvation through faith which is in Christ Jesus" (3:15). The salvation of our children is top priority, and what will lead them in the right direction is God's Word.

The Bible contains essential spiritual food. Start by feeding your children age-appropriate stories and promises from Scripture. Teach them God's commandments and their vital importance. Teach them about Jesus, His sacrifice, forgiveness, and grace. And, remember, you're not doing it alone. "I am with you always," is Jesus' enduring promise for mothers too.

Conversation

"Train up a child in the way he should go, and when he is old he will not depart from it" (Proverbs 22:6).

"Only take heed to yourself, and diligently keep yourself, lest you forget the things your eyes have seen, and lest they depart from your heart all the days of your life. And teach them to your children and your grandchildren" (Deuteronomy 4:9).

"All Scripture is given by inspiration of God, and is profitable for doctrine, for reproof, for correction, for instruction in righteousness" (2 Timothy 3:16).

---

2 http://www.dailymail.co.uk/news/article-2598149/Rwandan-woman-hand-chopped-baby-killed-genocide-20-years-ago-FRIENDS-man-did-it.html

Daily Reflection

Lessons I Learned:

(Reflect on opportunities for self-improvement.)

Personal Goal for Today:

(Identify one goal based on the reading.)

Today's Targets:

1.
2.
3.

(List three practical steps to help you reach your goal.)

Today I am thankful for:

(Write a short prayer of thanks to God for the blessings He has brought to you.)

Day 6

Miriam and the Bitter Cure

Karla Meza

> *"Pursue peace with all people, and holiness, without which no one will see the Lord: looking carefully lest anyone fall short of the grace of God; lest any root of bitterness springing up cause trouble, and by this many become defiled."* —Hebrews 12:14, 15

Have you ever struggled with bitterness? Have you questioned why others received honor but not you?

Her heart raced within her chest. She fought the urge to flee back to the relative safety of her slave quarters. But curiosity, love for her sibling, and a deep desire not to disappoint her mother kept Miriam's feet from running.

From the day Moses was born, Miriam quickly assumed her role as a protective older sister. This certainly wasn't surprising, especially considering the Egyptian decree that all Hebrew baby boys must be killed—a decree from which the entire family went to great lengths to protect baby Moses.

Miriam and her younger brother Aaron had godly parents who truly trusted God, but the king of Egypt, Pharaoh, hated her people. Because he was afraid of the Israelite slaves, he ordered that every baby boy be cast into the river.

This decree pierced the heart of Miriam's parents. They could not imagine losing their beautiful, extraordinary baby. Miriam helped her parents hide him for three long months. But after this time had passed, it became too dangerous to hide him in their home any longer. Miriam helped her mother as she made a papyrus basket and coated it with tar and pitch to make it waterproof.

Early one morning, she accompanied her mother to the crocodile-infested Nile River. When they arrived at the water, Miriam watched as her mother carefully placed the beloved baby in the basket and floated it on the river. The girl then stood cautiously at a distance to see what his fate would be.

Minutes stretched into hours, and Pharaoh's daughter arrived at the Nile to bathe—her female servants laughing and splashing nearby. Miriam caught her breath as the princess spied the beautiful basket caught amongst the reeds. She watched intently as a servant retrieved it and as the princess opened the lid. Miriam smiled in relief as the princess reached out, grasped the child, and spoke soothingly to him.

As if on cue, Miriam approached Pharaoh's daughter. "Shall I go and call a nurse for you from the Hebrew women, that she may nurse the child for you?" she inquired (Exodus 2:7). "Go," Pharaoh's daughter commanded. Nearly before the command had reached her ears, Miriam's feet were already pounding the hard dirt road, racing back to tell her family the good news.

If Miriam had only known that not only was she rescuing her baby brother, but also that someday this helpless little child would grow up to become the long hoped for rescuer of the Hebrew nation!

As an adult, Miriam also played an important role in the leadership of the Hebrew nation. The same strengths and quick discernment she demonstrated by the riverbed helped her in her new role over Israel. Miriam was the first to be named a "prophetess," inspired by His Holy Spirit to proclaim the will and purpose that God had revealed. Because of her calling as a prophetess and her close relationship with Moses, Miriam exerted great influence and power over the camp. But, sadly, this influence led to pride.

Miriam and Aaron began to criticize Moses for marrying an Ethiopian woman (Numbers 12:1). While she was ostensibly against the wife of Moses, the dissatisfaction ran much deeper. "'Has the LORD indeed spoken only through Moses? Has He not spoken through us also?' And the LORD heard it" (Numbers 12:2). In her criticism, Miriam was questioning God's wisdom in choosing Moses as the leader.

Daughters of God shares this insight: "In the affections of the people and the honor of Heaven she stood second only to Moses and Aaron. But the same evil that first brought discord in heaven sprang up in the heart of this woman of Israel, and she did not fail to find a sympathizer in her dissatisfaction. God had chosen Moses, and had put His Spirit upon him; and Miriam and Aaron, by their murmurings, were guilty of disloyalty, not only to their appointed leader, but to God Himself" (p. 33).

This bitterness and questioning of God did not go unnoticed by Him. Miriam was soon struck with leprosy, a certain death penalty. With horror, Aaron gazed upon his sister's stricken flesh. Quickly realizing the foolishness of their words, Aaron repented of his sin, and Moses cried to the Lord, "Please heal her, O God, I pray!" (Numbers 12:13). After a long week of isolation, Miriam was healed and returned to camp, greatly humbled by the experience.

Miriam, a gifted leader of God, quickly fell when she allowed bitterness to fill her heart. Bitterness may begin as just a small seed, but as it takes root, it soon controls us and others as our influence affects them—just as Miriam's influence affected Aaron.

How can we overcome bitterness? How can we experience healing in our own lives so that our pain isn't transferred to others through our angry words? Hebrews 12:2, 3 provides the answer: "Looking unto Jesus, the author and finisher of our faith, who for the joy that was set before Him endured the cross, despising the shame, and has sat down at the right hand of the throne of God. For consider Him who endured such hostility from sinners against Himself, lest you become weary and discouraged in your souls."

As we continue to keep our eyes fastened on Jesus—considering the sacrifice that He endured for our salvation—our own hearts will be healed and strengthened. Today, if you feel bitterness beginning to take root in your life, remember to look to Jesus, consider His life, and choose to spread only positive influences to others.

"Let no corrupt word proceed out of your mouth, but what is good for necessary edification, that it may impart grace to the hearers. . . . Let all bitterness, wrath, anger, clamor, and evil speaking be put away from you, with all malice. And be kind to one another, tenderhearted, forgiving one another, even as God in Christ forgave you" (Ephesians 4:29–32).

"For wrath kills a foolish man, and envy slays a simple one" (Job 5:2).

"Not returning evil for evil or reviling for reviling, but on the contrary blessing, knowing that you were called to this, that you may inherit a blessing" (1 Peter 3:9).

Daily Reflection

Lessons I Learned:

(Reflect on opportunities for self-improvement.)

Personal Goal for Today:

(Identify one goal based on the reading.)

Today's Targets:

1.
2.
3.

(List three practical steps to help you reach your goal.)

Today I am thankful for:

(Write a short prayer of thanks to God for the blessings He has brought to you.)

An Unlikely Vessel

Marsha Schick

"Their sins and their lawless deeds I will remember no more." —Hebrews 10:17

Have you ever made decisions that caused you to wonder how God could ever use you?

Armed soldiers of Jericho pounded on Rahab's door and shouted, "Bring out the men who have come to you, who have entered your house, for they have come to search out all the country" (Joshua 2:3). Rahab felt as if her heart would beat right out of her chest. She had never been approached by the king's guards like this. Were the foreigners in her home a threat to her safety? Was the king wrong about the intentions of these men? What should she do?

Rahab had heard about the wonders of the God of Israel. She learned how God had miraculously dried up the waters of the Red Sea—blazing a path where none had ever walked—so that the children of Israel could make it safely to the other side. The people of Jericho had also heard about the two kings of the Amorites and how they were utterly destroyed when they would not allow the Israelites to pass through their land peacefully. The fear and awesome power of a mighty God filled Rahab's heart, and she knew He was with these men. Consequently, this sobering realization meant that she was on the side opposing God. Rahab knew what she must do.

Quickly, she hid the two men on the roof of her house and answered the soldiers saying, "Yes, the men came to me, but I did not know where they were from. And it happened as the gate was being shut, when it was dark, that the men went out. Where the men went I do not know; pursue them quickly, for you may overtake them" (Joshua 2:4, 5). And with that she sent the king's soldiers on their way.

Rahab's mind was racing. Not only was the city of Jericho on territory that belonged to the Israelites, by God's promise, but Rahab had another predicament with which to grapple.

She had been living as a harlot. She had made a decision to take the priceless body God had given her and had degraded it to such a place where any amount of money was acceptable for it. How could she stand before a holy God?

She went to the spies she had hidden and petitioned them. She spoke of the miracle at the Red Sea and the destruction of the Amorites, telling them that her people had lost courage because of the Israelites. She expressed strong belief in the true God and begged the spies to show kindness toward her and her family, and to give her some token assuring her that their lives would be spared.

Rahab acknowledged and feared the God of heaven, so much so that she begged these men to swear by the Lord. She was relieved when the men agreed. When Rahab gave them final instructions for protection on their journey, the Israelite men handed her a scarlet cord to tie into the window of her house. In this way, the Israelites would know which house to bypass during the attack.

In Moses' day, during the first Passover, the Israelites too marked their homes with something scarlet. They were given careful instruction to mark the doorposts of their homes with the blood of a lamb so that no destructive plague would touch them. In doing so, the Israelites demonstrated faith in God and acknowledged His power to protect them from harm. "Thus also faith by itself, if it does not have works, is dead" (James 2:17).

In the same way, Rahab needed to bind the scarlet cord in faith so that none in her household would perish. The cord was a symbol of God's protection over Rahab's home. If she and her family wanted to live, they had to stay within the protective covering God had provided. But if they chose not to, their blood would be on their own heads (Joshua 2:19).

After the war on Jericho, Rahab, a former woman of sin, was welcomed into the Israelite family—and eventually went on to become an ancestor of Jesus! (See Matthew 1:5.) Rahab's scarred past did not prevent God from seeing her full potential. Indeed, she is commended in the Bible in Hebrews 11:31, which says, "By faith the harlot Rahab did not perish with those who did not believe, when she had received the spies with peace."

Today, God can work through us just as powerfully—as we, by faith, let go of our past and cling to Him. Right now, God has given us the opportunity to bind His scarlet cord into our hearts. Once we truly let God into every part of our lives, He is able to do marvelous things in us. The Bible says, "If anyone is in Christ, he is a new creation; old things have passed away; behold, all things have become new" (2 Corinthians 5:17).

You are so valuable to God that He sent Jesus, His only Son, to die on your behalf. What more could be given than the life of the Son of God? Scripture says that "He was wounded for our transgressions, He was bruised for our iniquities; the chastisement for our peace was upon Him, and by His stripes we are healed" (Isaiah 53:5). You are more precious to the Lord than you know! His grace and forgiveness is offered freely; it is yours for the asking. If you ever feel that you are inadequate before God, remember, "God demonstrates His own love toward us, in that while we were still sinners, Christ died for us" (Romans 5:8). Will you accept His excellent gift today?

Conversation

"The righteousness of God, through faith in Jesus Christ, to all and on all who believe. For there is no difference; for all have sinned and fall short of the glory of God, being justified freely by His grace through the redemption that is in Christ Jesus" (Romans 3:22–24).

"'Come now, and let us reason together,' says the LORD, 'Though your sins are like scarlet, they shall be as white as snow; though they are red like crimson, they shall be as wool'" (Isaiah 1:18).

"All that the Father gives Me will come to Me, and the one who comes to Me I will by no means cast out" (John 6:37).

Daily Reflection

Lessons I Learned:

(Reflect on opportunities for self-improvement.)

Personal Goal for Today:

(Identify one goal based on the reading.)

Today's Targets:

1.
2.
3.

(List three practical steps to help you reach your goal.)

Today I am thankful for:

(Write a short prayer of thanks to God for the blessings He has brought to you.)

The Weak Will be Strong

Dianne Cossentine

"God has chosen the foolish things of the world to put to shame the wise, and God has chosen the weak things of the world to put to shame the things which are mighty."—1 Corinthians 1:27

How do you respond when asked to do something out of your comfort zone?

Deborah settled down on her stool with a satisfied sigh and a warm smile. After taking in another long view of the valley, she pulled the basket of wicking fiber onto her lap.

After a busy morning, it was time to sit in the breeze under the palm tree and work on making wicks for the temple lamps. Deborah considered this work a high honor, so she took time to make the wicks thick and strong so that they would burn brightly. Her wicks were so well known that her husband, who delivered them to the priests, had been given the nickname "Lappidoth," which means "torches."

As she twisted the fibers together, she surveyed the nearby trail —a secondary road situated in the hill country of Ephraim between Ramah and Bethel—and prayed for her fellow Israelites as they wandered by. Her relationship with God had grown strong over the years, and He often gave her messages to share with the Israelites. On the other hand, His chosen people had once again turned to worshiping idols—and for twenty years, God had allowed the Canaanites to torment them. Bandits frequently attacked people on the main roads, so travelers often took less common trails like the one that passed by Deborah's palm tree.

These Israelite journeymen regularly stopped to rest in the shade with her. After the usual talk of weather, the conversation would turn to the latest news of attacks by the Canaanites. Deborah's genuine, compassionate attention, and the privacy afforded by the resting spot, gave them courage to tell her of their worries and troubles.

Her reputation for giving wise counsel spread, and soon people were coming to her palm tree specifically to have her resolve their disputes—so much so that God established her as a fourth judge of Israel. Deborah is the only female judge mentioned in the Bible, and she was the only judge who also served as a prophet.

Israel needed someone to bring the people together and to rescue them—for this purpose, God appointed Deborah. In that time and culture, it was highly unusual to have a female judge—or even a female prophet. It has been suggested that God placed a woman as a judge of Israel as a rebuke to the Israelites for failing to follow Him, yet the Bible provides no evidence of this.

When it was time to stop the madness of the Canaanite raiding parties, God instructed Deborah to have a man named Barak lead the Israelites to destroy the Canaanites and their leader, General Sisera. Since Barak was not as sure as Deborah of God's leading, he agreed to do it only if Deborah went along with him. Did Barak refuse to go into battle without her because he was frightened—or because he wanted to have God's prophet with him for assurance? Deborah told him, "I will surely go with you; nevertheless there will be no glory for you in the journey you are taking, for the LORD will sell Sisera into the hand of a woman" (Judges 4:9).

By this time, Israel did not have a well-equipped army, so Deborah and Barak led ten thousand poorly armed soldiers to Mount Tabor. By contrast, Sisera's army was well-equipped, including 900 iron chariots. They surely assumed the Israelites would be easily defeated, and they swarmed down to meet them at the River Kishon. But when God sent a rain storm, the river flooded the valley and those fierce chariots were soon stuck in mud. The Canaanites were left terrified, and Barak led the Israelites to kill every one of them—except Sisera, who jumped out of his chariot and fled for his life.

Sisera came to the tent of a woman named Jael, and she went out to meet him. She told him to not be afraid, to come inside her tent and find rest. She even gave him milk to drink and covered him with a blanket. Before he fell asleep, he asked her to stand at the door of the tent and to say he wasn't there if anyone came by looking for him. Soon he was sound asleep.

In those days, women were the ones who set up the tents, so Jael was skilled at using stakes and hammers. She also knew what the Canaanites had done to the Israelites for two decades and that Sisera was the general of the pagan army. Using the tools at hand, she seized the opportunity to bring the suffering of Israel to an end. She moved quietly to his side, took a deep breath, positioned a sharp tent stake at his temple, and struck it firmly with her hammer. The first blow killed him, but she drove the stake through his head and into the ground to confirm he would never rise again to harm anyone.

When Jael heard Barak running up to her tent, she met him outside and said, "Come, I will show you the man whom you seek" (Judges 4:22). Afterward, Deborah and Barak sang a victory song—recorded in Judges chapter 5—giving praise and glory to God and thanking Jael and the Israelite soldiers for their tremendous efforts.

When the "strong"—like Barak—don't do their jobs, God often brings in the "weak" to take care of business, often simply and efficiently. In the same way that God used young David to kill the giant Goliath and stop the Philistines, He used Deborah and Jael to kill Sisera and stop the Canaanites.

When you need to do something that is out of the ordinary, it is easy to think, "Anyone but me, Lord!" Don't tell Him, "I'll obey You *if* . . ." Go forward with the confidence that God will provide everything you need to conquer the task. Listen always for God's direction in whatever He has asked you to do. Follow Him and be sure to give Him the glory when He brings you the victory.

"Trust in the Lord with all your heart, and lean not on your own understanding; in all your ways acknowledge Him, and He shall direct your paths" (Proverbs 3:5, 6).

"Who knows whether you have come to the kingdom for such a time as this?" (Esther 4:14).

"[We] always ought to pray and not lose heart" (Luke 18:1).

Lessons I Learned:

(Reflect on opportunities for self-improvement.)

Personal Goal for Today:

(Identify one goal based on the reading.)

Today's Targets:

1.
2.
3.

(List three practical steps to help you reach your goal.)

Today I am thankful for:

(Write a short prayer of thanks to God for the blessings He has brought to you.)

I Will Not Leave Thee

Uliana Dzyndra

"Let your light so shine before men, that they may see your good works and glorify your Father in Heaven."—Matthew 5:16

Do you allow hardships to keep you from living a life of unselfishness and love?

Widowed and without an inheritance, Ruth would have been obligated to commit her life to following her mother-in-law, Naomi—who had every right to require the submission of her daughter-in-law according to her people's customs. However, since experiencing the death of her own husband, Naomi understood the sorrow facing Ruth. Without an inheritance of her own, and with unselfish love for Ruth, Naomi instead encouraged her to return to her own homeland. Naomi did not want to burden the life of Ruth with her own suffering and needs, so she liberated Ruth from any obligation.

Years earlier, to escape the famine in their homeland of Judah, Elimelech and Naomi traveled to the land of Moab with their two young sons. The sons married in Moab and lived there for ten years. Unfortunately, the two sons died as well, leaving Ruth and Orpah widows like their mother-in-law Naomi.

After hearing that God was providing food for her people in Judah, Naomi decided to return to her homeland. As the custom was, Ruth and Orpah followed Naomi along the way. Naomi understood the sacrifice these two young women were making in leaving their family. Naomi reasoned within herself, should their entire lives be afflicted by service and sorrow simply to relieve her own grief and provide for her needs? Lovingly, Naomi allowed each of them to return to her parents' home and start a new life. They were entirely free to choose what they would do.

As Orpah was saying goodbye, Ruth said, "Entreat me not to leave you . . . for wherever you go, I will go; and wherever you lodge, I will lodge; your people shall be my people, and your God, my God. Where you die, I will die, and there will I be buried. The Lord do so to me, and more also, if anything but death parts you and me" (Ruth 1:16, 17).

Wow! Ruth had been liberated, she had been given the freedom to go back to her family, yet she confidently affirmed her mother-in-law—she would not leave her, not unless death itself would part them. One commentary notes,

> Ruth could not bear to be separated from one whose beauty of character had inspired her own soul with high ideals and had given her something she felt was worth living for—even if she never again had a home of her own. . . . Here is the secret of Naomi's loveliness of character, of her appeal to Ruth—her first thoughts were ever of others. . . . In her life was reflected the likeness of Christ, who ordered His own life "for their sakes" (*SDA Bible Commentary*, Vol. 2, pg. 431).

Through Naomi's example, faith, and unselfishness, Ruth had come to the knowledge of the true God. She had seen His character reflected in Naomi and wanted this for herself. This is what made her leave her homeland and make such a daring commitment to someone from a different faith. She would do whatever necessary to follow Naomi to receive the blessing that continually flowed from her presence.

Many times, people may have a stronger relationship with their in-laws than they do with their own families. What makes the difference? Most likely, as in the example of Naomi, these godly people are Christ-like and care about the well-being of those around them. These are the kind of people that others want to be around. These are the kind of people that bring others into a closer relationship with Christ. Through Naomi's selfless love, Ruth was drawn closer to her—and thus to God.

Upon entering the land of Judah, Naomi created a stir among the people who recognized her. No doubt, she arrived with sorrow in her eyes and a loneliness that had not been seen in her previously. "Do not call me Naomi; call me Mara, for the Almighty has dealt very bitterly with me. I went out full, and the LORD has brought me home again empty. Why do you call me Naomi, since the LORD has testified against me, and the Almighty has afflicted me?" (Ruth 1:20, 21).

Yet, despite her discouragement, Naomi was obedient to God and had a strong relationship with Him. Ruth, in turn, was confident that Naomi knew what was best for her. When it came to preserving her mother-in-law's lineage, Ruth heeded Naomi's counsel. She married Boaz and through him bore a son, Obed, who was the grandfather of King David.

Naomi's example brought Ruth to the one true God. By her obedience, Ruth became the mother of kings, and her name is recorded in the very lineage of Jesus Christ. Without Naomi's example, Ruth would have returned to her homeland and never would have had this high honor. Every woman today can profit from studying the character of Naomi.

Very often in our lives, our difficulties seem to be more than we can bear. We can say, "Oh, you don't know my life; you have not been in my shoes." It may seem hard to focus on others and their struggles when we are so burdened with our own. But we have a wonderful promise that we can claim every day: "I can do all things through Christ who strengthens me" (Philippians 4:13).

Jesus encourages us to love our neighbors as ourselves (Mark 12:31). If we reach out in kindness in spite of our circumstances, Christ's character will be displayed in us and others will be brought to Him. "A kind, courteous Christian is the most powerful argument that can be produced in favor of Christianity" (*Gospel Workers*, p. 122).

"Let no one despise your youth, but be an example to the believers in word, in conduct, in love, in spirit, in faith, in purity" (1 Timothy 4:12).

"Whatever you want men to do to you, do also to them, for this is the Law and the Prophets" (Matthew 7:12).

"Let your light so shine before men, that they may see your good works and glorify your Father in heaven" (Matthew 5:16).

Lessons I Learned:

(Reflect on opportunities for self-improvement.)

Personal Goal for Today:

(Identify one goal based on the reading.)

Today's Targets:

1.

2.

3.

(List three practical steps to help you reach your goal.)

Today I am thankful for:

(Write a short prayer of thanks to God for the blessings He has brought to you.)

Day 10

A Remedy for Heart Trouble

Shemeka Bruton

"Weeping may endure for a night, but joy comes in the morning." —Psalm 30:5

Have you ever been brokenhearted?

Will this pain ever stop?, Ruth thought as her tears fell like rain.

Though the customary period of mourning had long since ended, the anguish that stemmed from losing her loving Mahlon, a faithful husband to her for a decade, had not. *How can I possibly go on without him?*

It was through Mahlon and his family that Ruth, a Moabite, had learned of the true God. As a Moabite, Ruth had likely grown up worshiping a god named Chemosh. He was the chief deity of her people, and his worship rites were known to be cruel and degrading—at times even involving human sacrifice. In contrast, she witnessed the worship of the God of heaven—Yahweh—as ennobling, uplifting, and peaceful. She made the ultimate decision to forsake the god of her fathers and embrace the God of the Hebrews.

Life had been good as the years rolled by, until the tragedy struck. Both Ruth and her sister-in-law Orpah, also a Moabite, were now forced to confront the reality of widowhood as both of their husbands were laid to rest. Ruth's dreams of a long, happy life together, accompanied by the joy of children and later grandchildren, were dashed to pieces. No doubt, in the midst of her sorrow, she was tempted to doubt the love of this God she had adopted. *Is this the reward of serving this God? Is this how the God of love treats His followers?* Have you ever struggled with such thoughts during times of difficulty, loneliness, or bereavement?

Likewise, bereft of the loving companionship of a husband, as well as her two sons, another woman named Naomi made the decision to leave the land of Moab and return to her home country—a land called Judah. She bid her daughters-in-law—Ruth and Orpah—to return to their own ancestral families as well. Heartbroken, Ruth now faced separation from a other-in-law she dearly loved. Though Ruth was not an Israelite, Naomi had always treated er with kindness, as if Ruth were her own daughter.

Surely many worrying thoughts swirled through Ruth's mind—*What is left for me in 'oab, especially since I have forsaken Chemosh? And how will Naomi survive alone without a usband or sons? Who will help her—especially when she's old.*

While Orpah chose to turn back to her people, Ruth clung to Naomi, saying, "Entreat e not to leave you, or to turn back from following after you; for wherever you go, I will go; nd wherever you lodge, I will lodge; your people shall be my people, and your God, my God" Ruth 1:16).

Often when disaster hits, our thoughts focus on our affliction. We feel nothing but our wn pain; see nothing but our own hardship; and hear nothing but our own sobs. Yet, believe or not, many around us have wounds that cut deeper than our own. What would happen if e turned our thoughts from ourselves and sought, instead, to lift the burdens of another? hough Ruth was suffering the pain of loss, so was Naomi—and she had even lost her nly sons.

The two widowed women made their way to Judah, about 45 miles from Moab. The trip kely took them seven to ten days on foot through rugged, hostile terrain. According to the ible, they returned at the beginning of the barley harvest—sometime in the spring. Being hildless and without husbands, both women had to find a means of support. Ruth decided go out to the wheat fields to glean what hired reapers left behind while harvesting. God, in is great mercy for those less fortunate, made provision in the Levitical law that some grain hould be left behind during the harvest so that the poor and the stranger could collect it. (See eviticus 19:9, 10.)

In the providence of God, Ruth wound up in the field of Boaz, a man who happened o be a relative of Naomi. Boaz had great wealth and influence. When he inquired about the tranger and learned about her, he showed great favor toward her. We're told exactly why in uth 2:11, 12:

> It has been fully reported to me, all that you have done for your mother-in-law since the death of your husband, and how you have left your father and your mother and the land of your birth, and have come to a people whom you did not know before. The Lord repay your work, and a full reward be given you by the Lord God of Israel, under whose wings you have come for refuge.

Boaz then directed his workers to leave extra for Ruth to collect and commanded them not to touch her. Ruth was humbled, and no doubt charmed, that this wealthy stranger shoulc show such kindness to her, a Moabite.

Naomi, hearing about the generosity of Boaz, saw in him an opportunity for Ruth to onc again enjoy the love and companionship that God had designed the marriage relationship to bring. Following the careful instruction of her mother-in-law, Ruth went on to become the happy wife of Boaz. Even more than that, she became the mother of Obed, who was the fathe of Jesse, who was the father of David the King. And from this lineage came Jesus the Messiah!

We can hardly fathom how ministering to the needs of others will minister to us in return. Is your heart broken? Seek out one whose heart is more shattered than your own, and in the power of God, seek to be a source of blessing while selflessly hoping for nothing in return. Jesus, our wounded Healer, sought the good of others even while dying on a cross (See John 19:26, 27.)

Will you follow His loving example in your everyday life?

"The generous soul will be made rich, and he who waters will also be watered himself" (Proverbs 11:25).

"Let each of you look out not only for his own interests, but also for the interests of others" (Philippians 2:4).

"Whoever has this world's goods, and sees his brother in need, and shuts up his heart from him, how does the love of God abide in him?" (1 John 3:17).

essons I Learned:

____

____

____

____

eflect on opportunities for self-improvement.)

ersonal Goal for Today:

____

____

____

dentify one goal based on the reading.)

oday's Targets:

- ____
- ____
- ____

ist three practical steps to help you reach your goal.)

oday I am thankful for:

____

____

____

____

Write a short prayer of thanks to God for the blessings He has brought to you.)

Day 11

In Prosperity and Adversity

Pam Lascoe

"I take pleasure in infirmities, in reproaches, in needs, in persecutions, in distresses, for Christ's sake. For when I am weak, then am I strong."—2 Corinthians 12:10

Have you ever wanted anything in life so much that you couldn't eat, sleep, or even think of anything else?

We've all been there at some point in life! Maybe it was a job, your health, children, finances, some person who troubled you, or another stressful situation—and you've spent hours and hours pleading with the Lord to change your circumstances. Perhaps sometimes it seems as if He hasn't heard even one of your prayers.

Maybe you're in the throes of some heart-wrenching experience now, feeling as if God just doesn't have time for you, and you're wondering why He hasn't answered your pleas for relief from the stress. I've been there, on more than one occasion, ready to give up and turn away from the Savior—simply because I'm tired of pleading for my cause.

Then there are those well-meaning folks who think they have all the right answers for your situation. Boy, do they ever make me want to scream! But, the right thing to do is just smile and say, "Thank you," and continue with your day, just like Hannah. Amazing and beautiful though Hannah's prayer may be, the layers of 1 Samuel and her incredible story offer so much more in our daily Christian walk than we typically see on the surface. One thing that strikes me between the eyes is: How do I respond with grace and restraint when struggling with life, especially when being taunted, belittled, or accused, like Hannah always seemed to be? Let's dig deeper together and see.

Years had passed, and after countless hours of pleading with the Lord, she was still unable to carry a child. Hannah, never disagreeing with her husband Elkanah's decision to take another wife, silently carried the burden of being barren for years. Although his second wife as able to give him the joy of sons and daughters, this decision brought great division and 'ief into the family home. You see, Peninnah was exceedingly bitter toward her husband's first ife, mocking Hannah continually for her lack of children. It seemed that Peninnah especially creased her spiteful insults during the times when the family went up together to Shiloh to lebrate the annual feasts—times when the family was supposed to be joyful.

Elkanah was a Levite, and although he wasn't an active priestly participant in the feast, e was devout and required of his family the same pious nature. Unfortunately, bringing these ivided factions of his home together only allowed for more opportunity to remind Peninnah, rough the sacrificial services and feasts, of the deep love Elkanah carried for Hannah. This urred her venomous affronts to grow more fervent, breaking Hannah's spirit and bringing er lower than ever before.

Without retaliation, poor Hannah allowed Peninnah to continue throwing insults her 'ay, and incredibly, Hannah never complained to her husband—from what we read in 1 amuel—about her adversary's behavior. She never threw back insults or claimed that their usband loved her more—perhaps because, during their feasts, he would give Hannah "a ouble portion, for he loved Hannah, although the LORD had closed her womb" (1 Samuel 1:5).

Hannah was so distraught she could neither eat of the good food nor drink. So what do ou think she did? "She was in bitterness of soul, and prayed to the LORD and wept in anguish" Samuel 1:10). She went to the temple and prayed to God! But while she intently prayed, e high priest, Eli, accused her of being drunk! Are you kidding? It wasn't enough that this ther woman in her life had been badgering her for years, but now the high priest accuses her f drunkenness!

How many of us would have snapped in the same situation? However, Hannah showed li full respect and simply shared with him her situation. Wow!

Every day we are bombarded with people and situations that are difficult to bear, and is how we react to them that shows the world who we are as Christians. We can choose to e quick to respond—which we often do—or model the way Hannah conducted her life: by oing to the Lord and finding strength in Him. We can stop our feeble attempts at making nings work in our own way—which is typically wrong—and instead show restraint and espond with respect.

When contemplating the word "restraint," we often think of something that orcibly restricts our movement or actions. In the eyes of the world, restraint has negative onnotations, but when seen through the story and life of Hannah, it is a lovely character trait hat I wish I had more of—especially when being condemned or falsely accused.

Because Hannah gave the situation to God and trusted that *He* would handle *all* aspects of it, she was at peace.

That same peace is well within our grasp every day as well! All we have to do is ask. Using a heart of restraint and faith, we can also have the Lord's help in trying situations. He can and will change our attitudes, proving that we can have peace in all adverse situations. Then our countenances, too, will no longer be sad! There are incredible lessons to learn from Hannah's story. With God's help, we can live with restraint and joy in both prosperity and adversity.

What a great and loving God we are able to love and serve!

Conversation

"In the day of prosperity be joyful, but in the day of adversity consider: God also hath set the one over against the other, to the end that man should find nothing after him" (Ecclesiastes 7:14 KJV).

"I have learned in whatever state I am, to be content: . . . I have learned both to be full and to be hungry, both to abound and to suffer need. I can do all things through Christ who strengthens me" (Philippians 4:11–13).

"Trust in the LORD with all your heart, and lean not on your own understanding; in all your ways acknowledge Him, and He shall direct your paths" (Proverbs 3:5, 6).

Daily Reflection

Lessons I Learned:

(Reflect on opportunities for self-improvement.)

Personal Goal for Today:

(Identify one goal based on the reading.)

Today's Targets:

1.
2.
3.

(List three practical steps to help you reach your goal.)

Today I am thankful for:

(Write a short prayer of thanks to God for the blessings He has brought to you.)

Power of a Woman's Words

Michelle Kiss

"Death and life are in the power of the tongue, and those who love it will eat its fruit." —Proverbs 18:21

Have you ever wished you knew just what to say at the right time?

Abigail's day began just before the break of dawn, yet a few hours in she was overwhelme with all the preparations for the evening's festivities. It was sheep-shearing season in Israel—an event that took place between the months of May and June. Her husband, Nabal, was already out in the fields with his men.

Needing a few moments to herself, Abigail decided to steal away from all the busyness of the morning. As she stood outside with her eyes closed, she could feel the kiss of the summer sun on her face, the cool breeze dancing through her hair. With her eyes still closed, her other senses kicked in. She could hear the sweet songs of birds, the rustling of the leaves through the trees . . . and something she did not expect. In the distance, she heard a man calling out for her. As he drew nearer, she could sense the urgency in his voice. She opened her eyes to see a terrified look on his face. It was one of Nabal's servants, and the news he was bringing cast a dark shadow on the day's mood.

While Nabal and his servants had been going about their work in Carmel, young men from David's army had approached them. These soldiers had brought greetings from David, who was camping in Paran with six hundred men. They also asked Nabal if he would provide them with some provisions, as they were running low. But Nabal, being the selfish, foolish man that he was, had only insults for them; he had sent them away empty-handed.

The disheartened men went back to David to relay the stinging message. It was a huge insult, because David had taken it upon himself to protect Nabal's shepherds and his entire flock of sheep from bandits and Ishmaelites.

The servant informed Abigail, "The men were very good to us, and we were not hurt, nor did we miss anything as long as we accompanied them. . . . They were a wall to us both by night and day, all the time we were with them keeping the sheep" (1 Samuel 25:15, 16). The protection Nabal received from David and his men was the reason he was so successful in Carmel. But Nabal showed no appreciation for what David had done.

When David heard the news, he was furious and ordered his best men to arm themselves for a fight—with the promise that Nabal and all his male servants would be dead by morning. Abigail knew she had to act quickly to save her foolish husband and entire household from certain death. She said nothing to Nabal, but sought to do what was right—whatever the cost. Without hesitation, this woman of wisdom gathered food for David and his men—"two hundred loaves of bread, two skins of wine, five sheep already dressed, five seahs of roasted grain, one hundred clusters of raisins, and two hundred cakes of figs, and loaded them on donkeys" (1 Samuel 25:18). She told her servants to go ahead of her and deliver the gifts; she would follow soon after.

The Bible doesn't mention what Abigail did after she sent the servants ahead, but I can imagine that she ran back to the house to get herself ready—fixing her hair, applying a favorite scented oil, and putting on her finest apparel. After all, she was going to meet the future king of Israel and wanted to make a good impression.

When Abigail caught up to David, she got off her donkey and bowed before him, her face to the ground—showing him the utmost respect. What an incredible contrast to the way her husband Nabal treated him! Abigail apologized for her husband's foolish actions and took the blame upon herself, asking David to have mercy upon her, and to accept the gift she had sent as a peace offering. She asked David not to pursue the course he was on, but to trust that the Lord would fight his battles and take care of Nabal in his own time. "The Lord will certainly make for my lord an enduring house, because my lord fights the battles of the Lord, and evil is not found in you throughout your days" (1 Samuel 25:28).

Abigail convinced David that the course of action he was about to take was not one the Lord wanted. She was careful with her words and courageously trusted that God would act in a mighty way. She had spared her household from certain disaster and David from committing a sin that would've put a stain on his good reputation. When Abigail returned home, the celebration was already underway. Nabal was drunk and unaware of the tragedy that could have taken place had it not been for the wisdom and quick action of his wife.

In the morning, when Nabal had sobered up, Abigail decided to tell him what she had done. Upon hearing the distressing news, Nabal's heart gave out and ten days later, he died.

When David heard the news of Nabal's death, he praised God for sparing him from taking matters into his own hands. David then sent word to Abigail and asked if she would be his wife. Abigail quickly and humbly accepted his marriage proposal.

The power of a woman's words changed the course of David's life. In return, it changed Abigail's life and the lives of those around her. Abigail's choices showed strength and courage. She was beautiful inside and out and greatly respected in her home and community. She was a woman of wisdom, intelligence, and faith. She showed restraint with her words and was submissive to a foolish and ungodly man who cared only about himself; in the end, she prevailed.

We can use our words to disparage and tear others down, or we can use them to bless, uplift, and influence generations to come. Let us encourage one another, and pray that God will help us use our words to build others up for His glory.

"Pleasant words are like a honeycomb, sweetness to the soul and health to the bones" (Proverbs 16:24).

"A soft answer turns away wrath, but a harsh word stirs up anger. The tongue of the wise uses knowledge rightly, but the mouth of fools pours forth foolishness" (Proverbs 15:1, 2).

"Walk in wisdom toward those who are outside, redeeming the time. Let your speech always be with grace, seasoned with salt, that you may know how you ought to answer each one" (Colossians 4:5, 6).

Lessons I Learned:

(Reflect on opportunities for self-improvement.)

Personal Goal for Today:

(Identify one goal based on the reading.)

Today's Targets:

1.
2.
3.

(List three practical steps to help you reach your goal.)

Today I am thankful for:

(Write a short prayer of thanks to God for the blessings He has brought to you.)

The Quest of Royalty

Reba Jones

"Receive my instruction, and not silver, and knowledge rather than choice gold; for wisdom is better than rubies, and all the things one may desire cannot be compared with her." —Proverbs 8:10, 11

How far would you go to find the answer to your deepest longing?

Before her eager, weary eyes, the arid landscape stretched to the distant horizon. Miles passed beneath her jeweled feet, echoing back in the *thump, thump, thump* of her royal entourage. Every step of her life had brought her to this: the quest of a lifetime. And though the dust settled heavy as a monsoon rain against her skin, it could not thwart her determination.

At long last, the royal procession snaked like a string of black pearls down the streets of Jerusalem. Then, beyond stately columns of ornately carved marble, the queen's searching gaze finally rested on King Solomon.

For millennia, royals voyaged over land and sea searching for the wealth of foreign lands. Scholars believe that the Queen of Sheba traveled to Jerusalem from the region we now know as Ethiopia and Yemen—a trek of nearly two thousand miles. The journey by caravan lasted approximately thirty-five days. And the prize of her expedition? Wisdom.

Hers was a land teeming with culture abounding with spiritual ideas. Yet, despite her lavish surroundings, questions from within her heckled—as vexing as the sand flies that hung low in the evening air. And despite the wealth of her household, those yearnings of her inmost heart had remained unsatisfied. For her, no treasure could be valued above understanding.

Reports of the great King Solomon had reached her distant home, yet who could believe what was said about him? Hope had thrilled within her. Could this be the one from whom she might receive wisdom? She knew from the start that no matter how far away it was, she must journey in search of this prize.

Glimmers of gold mingled with fragrant African spices as the queen poured out every testing question in her heart. Burdens that for years had plagued her vanished in the light of divine insight. Everywhere she looked she could see the effects of wisdom. Breathless with astonishment and joy she exclaimed,

> Happy are your men and happy are these your servants, who stand continually before you and hear your wisdom! Blessed be the LORD your God, who delighted in you, setting you on His throne to be king for the LORD your God! Because your God has loved Israel . . . therefore he made you king over them, to do justice and righteousness (2 Chronicles 9:7, 8).

So Solomon gave the Queen of Sheba all that she desired . . . *and more*.

Had there ever been such a search for wisdom more diligent than the quest of this ancient queen? Throughout history, hearts the world over have throbbed with unanswered questions. Whether faint or resounding, we may each hear, somewhere within us, a yearning for something more than what lies within our natural reach. The question is—how far do *we* go and how diligent is *our* search for wisdom?

Jesus said, "The queen of the South will rise up in the judgment with this generation and condemn it, for she came from the ends of the earth to hear the wisdom of Solomon; and indeed a greater than Solomon is here" (Matthew 12:42).

Just think of it: Jewish leaders in Jesus' time had the very source and substance of wisdom walking among them, day after day, yet they neglected to receive it. Maybe we are not so much unlike them. In an age where we can circle the globe in a few days and information is as close as a touchscreen, just how diligent is our search and how extensive our inquiry?

The truth is that, incredibly, Christ has already taken the longest and most arduous trek imaginable to provide the answer to our deepest longing. We are not destined to wander the arid landscape of complacency or doubt.

It is for us, the royal heirs of the work of Jesus Christ, to seek diligently for the wisdom that comes from above. It must be *our* quest to seek out the One who has become to us wisdom, righteousness, sanctification, and redemption. For only in His kingly gift can we receive all that *we* desire . . . and more!

When the Queen of Sheba made her way into Solomon's Jerusalem, she found more than an earthly kingdom in operation. His was a kingdom ruled by the principles of the one true God. According to Scripture, this wisdom extended to the order of his home, the food on his table, and the treatment of his employees. It was the spirit of wisdom permeating Solomon's life and reign that most won the queen's admiration. She was drawn to acknowledge the true King of Israel, the who had set Solomon on the earthly throne. Through him, she was introduced to the Creator and the happiness and harmony that result from knowing Him. He *is* wisdom, and from Him comes knowledge and understanding.

This same experience may be ours today—as we take up the royal quest that now beckons to us from the pages of God's Word. Is it *your* desire to commit to the quest for wisdom? How far will *you* go to find the answer to your deepest longing?

"The fear of the Lord is the beginning of wisdom, and the knowledge of the Holy One is understanding" (Proverbs 9:10).

"Then you will call upon Me and go and pray to Me, and I will listen to you. And you will seek Me and find Me, when you search for Me with all your heart. I will be found by you says the Lord" (Jeremiah 29:12–14).

"If you cry out for discernment, and lift up your voice for understanding, if you seek her as silver, and search for her as for hidden treasures; then you will understand the fear of the Lord, and find the knowledge of God. For the Lord gives wisdom; from His mouth come knowledge and understanding; He stores up sound wisdom for the upright" (Proverbs 2:3–7).

Lessons I Learned:

(Reflect on opportunities for self-improvement.)

Personal Goal for Today:

(Identify one goal based on the reading.)

Today's Targets:

1.
2.
3.

(List three practical steps to help you reach your goal.)

Today I am thankful for:

(Write a short prayer of thanks to God for the blessings He has brought to you.)

Day 14

The Smallest Sacrifice

Shemeka Bruton

"I know the thoughts that I think toward you, says the Lord, thoughts of peace and not of evil, to give you a future and a hope." —Jeremiah 29:11

Have you ever felt like God was asking too much of you?

How will I know her?" he no doubt wondered. God's instruction to Elijah had been specific: "Arise, go to Zarephath, which belongs to Sidon, and dwell there. See, I have commanded a widow there to provide for you" (1 Kings 17:9).

The nation of Israel, God's chosen people, had once again turned from Him to worship the false gods of the heathen nations around them. King Ahab and Queen Jezebel had been ready tools in the hands of Satan to promote and encourage this departure. Their apostasy had reached such a fever-pitch that God had to send the prophet Elijah to deliver the message, "As the Lord God of Israel lives, before whom I stand, there shall not be dew nor rain these years, except at my word" (1 Kings 17:1).

God is so merciful. He often sustains and provides for us even in the midst of our disobedience. The very blessings He bestows upon us we too often turn around and use against Him in deeds of sin and selfishness. He blesses us with money, and we rob Him of His due. He blesses us with a companion, and we make that person an idol in our lives—neglecting to spend time with Him. He blesses us with a new job or promotion, and we brag about how *our* ingenuity, *our* qualifications, *our* hard work alone secured this for us—neglecting to give Him the glory. Thankfully, God is patient and bears long with us; however, as so vividly illustrated in the nation of Israel's history, continued disobedience surely brings consequences.

The realities of the drought were felt not only by the Israelites but also by the nations surrounding them. It's so often true that when we turn away from God, we aren't the only ones affected.

Elijah had been sustained by water he drank from the brook Cherith and by food ıat was miraculously delivered to him by ravens. But, eventually, the brook dried up. Now ıe prophet, God's mouthpiece, the one that was being obedient, was affected by the onsequences of the nation's apostasy.

Trials don't only come to the disobedient. Trials are a part of life. We have an enemy, nd we are warned that he "walks about like a roaring lion, seeking whom he may devour" 1 Peter 5:8). God shields us from much, but our faith will be tested.

With his water source gone, Elijah had to move on, and then came God's command to o to Zarephath. We don't know exactly how long a journey this was, but it would have surely een long enough for Elijah to become quite hungry and thirsty. He needed to find this widow. ut how was he to *know* he had found the right person? It's not likely that she was the *only* vidow in Zarephath.

Interestingly, the Scriptures record no physical description of this woman, nor even o much as her name. But God puts more stock in the beauty of our character than in our utward appearance. What she looked like, where she lived, even her name, were not nearly as mportant as who she was on the inside.

On that fateful day, no doubt feeling forgotten, she was collecting sticks. How would t feel to collect sticks to prepare the last meal for yourself and your only child? Most of us vill never know. As she went about her mournful task, she may have thought herself to be ompletely forgotten in the mind of God. Little did she know how abundant His thoughts were oward her.

The prophet, a stranger, requested water. Forgetting her own needs, she went dutifully to ulfill his request. When he asked for a morsel of bread, she said,

> "As the Lord your God lives, I do not have bread, only a handful of flour in a bin, and a little oil in a jar; and see, I am gathering a couple of sticks that I may go in and prepare it for myself and my son, that we may eat it, and die." And Elijah said to her, "Do not fear; go and do as you have said, but make me a small cake from it first, and bring it to me; and afterward make some for yourself and your son. For thus says the Lord God of Israel: 'The bin of flour shall not be used up, nor shall the jar of oil run dry, until the day the Lord sends rain on the earth'" (1 Kings 17:12–14).

This was a great test of faith! But, what was God really asking her to give up? Only the prospect of certain death. What did she have to lose? Even if she and her son ate that last meal, they would have eventually died from starvation. If Elijah had turned out to be a swindler and ran off after eating it, they would have still died from starvation. She had virtually nothing to lose in giving Elijah her last bit of food. If he proved to be a true prophet of God, she would have food sufficient for her needs.

Today, what is God asking *us* to give up? The prospect of eternal death. What do we have to lose? Our worldly possessions? A relationship, possibly? A sought-after job, potentially? But what are these things in the light of eternity? In comparison, what God is asking us to sacrifice is small. Incomparable. "God does not require us to give up anything that it is for our best interest to retain" (*Steps to Christ*, pg. 46).

When you put things in their proper perspective, God is offering us the greatest gift for the smallest sacrifice. This doesn't negate the fact that there will be a struggle, but when we cross the threshold of the pearly gates into that glorious eternal city, the sacrifices that we made here will appear so small that we won't even be able to call them to mind.

May we ever keep before us the thought of the greatest sacrifice ever made with the promise of the greatest reward ever given.

"The wages of sin is death, but the gift of God is eternal life in Christ Jesus our Lord" (Romans 6:23).

"To console those who mourn in Zion, to give them beauty for ashes, the oil of joy for mourning, the garment of praise for the spirit of heaviness; that they may be called trees of righteousness, the planting of the Lord, that He may be glorified" (Isaiah 61:3).

"Jesus answered and said to her, 'If you knew the gift of God, and who it is who says to you, "Give Me a drink," you would have asked Him, and He would have given you living water' " (John 4:10).

Daily Reflection

essons I Learned:

ʀeflect on opportunities for self-improvement.)

ersonal Goal for Today:

dentify one goal based on the reading.)

oday's Targets:

ist three practical steps to help you reach your goal.)

oday I am thankful for:

Nrite a short prayer of thanks to God for the blessings He has brought to you.)

A Small Jar of Oil

Natalia Dzyndra

"Cast your burden on the Lord, and He shall sustain you; He shall never permit the righteous to be moved." —Psalm 55:22

Have you ever wondered if God could provide for your needs when you had nothing left?

What are we going to do? Our father's debt is so big, we could never repay it! If we leave Mother to become slaves, what will happen to her? How will she survive?" The brothers were out of options, and their future seemed grim. They had lost all hope. It was time to start packing their few belongings and say their goodbyes.

Their widowed mother, overhearing their conversation, wasn't about to lose hope. Her husband had been one of the prophets. They had witnessed the power of God's miracles. They were devoted believers, and they knew God. With nothing left of her own might, the widow sought help from the mighty prophet Elisha, crying out to him: "Your servant my husband is dead, and you know that your servant feared the Lord. And the creditor is coming to take my two sons to be his slaves" (2 Kings 4:1).

The widow simply stated her situation. She could have asked for gold and silver; she could have asked for horses or sheep; she could have asked for anything. But she didn't. She just brought her trouble to the prophet and laid it at his feet. The widow didn't come to him hoping that he might be able to help her. She came in faith, that as God's representative, he would help her. She didn't know how, but that was of little importance to her. She was willing to do whatever necessary to keep her sons at home with her.

When the widow brought her hardship to Elisha, he asked, "Tell me, what do you have in the house?" (v. 2). Maybe the widow was surprised at the question, but often God will use whatever we have in order to help us.

All the widow had left in her house was a jar of oil. In her day, oil was very useful and cessary, but she only had a small amount left in her jar. However, she told the prophet, rhaps feeling that it was insignificant and hardly worth mentioning.

Do you remember the story of the boy who brought all he had to Jesus—a meager nch of five loaves and two fish? The Lord multiplied that small contribution and fed over 000 men, not including women and children. In a similar way, the Lord multiplied the idow's jar of oil.

Elisha told the widow to go and borrow vessels from all her neighbors. "Do not gather st a few," was his instruction. If she was coming to God for help, believing and trusting that would, then she needed to be prepared to receive His help. Elisha continued, "When you ve come in, you shall shut the door behind you and your sons; then pour [the one jar of oil] to all those vessels, and set aside the full ones" (2 Kings 4:4).

Can you imagine being in the widow's shoes? Wouldn't you question Elisha? How is it ossible for one small jar of oil to fill an entire room full of vessels? At this point, the widow uld have easily said, "Forget it! This is ridiculous! I am not going to make a fool of myself." ow often do we question God when He tells us to do something that, to us, seems ridiculous?

The widow could have responded to Elisha with skepticism; she could have borrowed ly a couple of vessels. But she had seen the power of God that transcended human nderstanding; she had witnessed His ability to take care of His children.

As the widow and her sons went from neighbor to neighbor, borrowing not a few ssels, they might have been wondering if what they were doing was in vain. But as they ut the door behind them and began to fill those vessels, their expressions began to change. ney felt a rush of unimaginable joy and amazement. The oil from the small jar kept flowing. e vessels were being filled to the brim, one after another, after another, after another. They arched for more empty vessels and could not find any. If only they had gone to a few more eighbors, the oil would have kept flowing!

As the brothers marveled over the miracle they had witnessed, the widow went back Elisha to tell him what had happened. He then instructed her, "Go, sell the oil and pay your ebt; and you and your sons live on the rest" (v. 7). The distressing problem that had seemed so omplex came to a simple resolution in the hands of the Lord.

Sometimes we come to God asking Him for something specific or extraordinary, omething we think will help us through our Christian walk. But as this story illustrates, we ould do well to simply come to God and tell Him our struggles, expecting Him to answer us His way and in His own time. For we know "it is God who works in you both to will and to do for His good pleasure" (Philippians 2:13). He is ready to give you great gifts (Matthew 7:11). I may be in ways you could never have imagined.

God is not limited. He is able to use whatever we have, even when there is nothing left. In fact, when we are at our poorest and weakest, God can work the greatest miracles. He doesn't need much; if all you have is a small jar of oil, He will use that to bless you. He is ready and willing to provide for our needs, but we must come to Him and allow Him to use us. We must give ourselves fully to Him and then do as He instructs. This is not the time to doubt and question; we must have faith that He will help.

Will you trust God today to help you in your trials? Give them all to Him and believe He will take care of you.

"Do not worry about tomorrow, for tomorrow will worry about its own things. Sufficient for the day is its own trouble" (Matthew 6:34).

"I, the LORD your God, will hold your right hand, saying to you, 'Fear not, I will help you' " (Isaiah 41:13).

"Be anxious for nothing, but in everything by prayer and supplication, with thanksgiving, let your requests be made known to God; and the peace of God, which surpasses all understanding, will guard your hearts and minds through Christ Jesus" (Philippians 4:6, 7).

ssons I Learned:

eflect on opportunities for self-improvement.)

rsonal Goal for Today:

lentify one goal based on the reading.)

day's Targets:

ist three practical steps to help you reach your goal.)

day I am thankful for:

Vrite a short prayer of thanks to God for the blessings He has brought to you.)

Day 16

A Mother's Plea

Diane McSherry

"As the LORD lives, and as your soul lives, I will not leave you!"—2 Kings 2:2

Have you ever lost someone or something that you passionately loved?

It had started out as a perfect day. She had watched as her young son followed his daddy into the fields to work. He was growing so fast, this miracle child. He was a gift from God—thank you from Prophet Elisha and his servant Gehazi for building them a room and providing a home to stay in while traveling down the long road. The boy was a precious blessing.

As the morning wore on, she heard the servant running up the road. He gently carried a bundle in his arms. As he drew closer, she saw that it was her little boy. The child had complained of pain in his head, so his dad had sent him home. She gathered him to her and sat rocking the precious child on her lap. What could she do to help stop his pain? She held him close to her heart, praying that he would feel better. She had tried all the known remedies, but now her child peacefully slept. Not the sleep that she would be able to rouse him from, but the deep sleep of death.

Gently, she carried her child up the stairs into the prophet's room. She carefully laid him on the bed and covered him as she would any other time he was asleep. He was no longer in pain, but the pain in her heart tore at her as she turned and closed the door behind her. Now she was on a mission. There was no time to waste. She had faith in the God of Elisha, who had given her this precious son when she had been barren for so long. She had to reach the man of God so he could raise up her son.

When her husband asked if everything was okay, she answered with a determined "All is well." He wondered why she was taking a servant and donkey and heading out to see the prophet; it was neither Sabbath nor the New Moon. But there was no time to explain. She had get going! The servant must have understood her urgency when she requested that he ride ıst—the faster the better.

Looking out in the distance, Elisha saw a cloud of dust on the road and realized someone ıust be on an urgent mission. As they drew near, Elisha recognized the woman of Shunem and ith great concern sent Gehazi out to meet her. "Is everything well?" he implored.

"All is well," was her answer. She knew that Gehazi cared for her son, but it was not ehazi that the determined mother had come to see. She couldn't stop to explain her mission ut pressed on toward Elisha.

When she came to the man of God, she caught him by his feet. Gehazi tried to push her way, but the gentle prophet cautioned him to leave her. God had not revealed to Elisha why he had come, but the admonition to his servant Gehazi showed the compassion he felt—for er soul was in deep distress.

"Did I ask for a son?" Her pleading face showed the deep anguish she felt. Elisha didn't aste one moment as he told Gehazi to take his staff and go. He instructed him not to greet nyone that greeted him along the way, but to hurry to the child. Once there, he was to lay the taff on the face of the child. Gehazi left and did as he was told.

But the mother would not leave with Elisha's servant. She had come to bring the rophet home to awaken her dead child. She had heard him tell of the miracles that had been erformed by God. Elisha was a gentle teacher, and she knew that the God he served cared for er child. With pleading she said, "As the Lord lives, and as your soul lives, I will not leave you!"

Those familiar words that he had once spoken were now being repeated back to him. ctually, Elisha had spoken them three times. They were the exact words he had spoken to the rophet Elijah when he had refused to leave his side on that final day when Elijah was caught p in a fiery chariot. This mother had listened to the story and had used his very words to show hat she needed him for this miracle. So he arose and followed her.

Gehazi had gone on ahead and followed the directions of the prophet, but there had een no change in the child. When Elisha arrived, he found the child lying dead on his bed. He vent into the room, shut the door, and prayed to the Lord. What a heartfelt prayer that must ave been—for Elisha had spent countless hours with this little child and his parents.

After he prayed, the prophet Elisha lay on the child, putting his mouth on the child's nouth, eyes on his eyes, and hands on his hands. He stretched himself on the child and the lesh of the child became warm. He then walked back and forth in the home and again went ıp and stretched himself on the child. The boy sneezed. Seven times that little boy sneezed! The sleeping child had awakened!

The prophet Elisha asked Gehazi to call the mom to gather up her child. She went in, fell at Elisha's feet, and bowed to the ground in gratitude for what God had done. After this, she picked up her son and went out. Her precious son had been raised from the dead!

> So was the faith of this woman rewarded. Christ, the great Life-giver, restored her son to her. In like manner will His faithful ones be rewarded, when, at His coming, death loses its sting and the grave is robbed of the victory it has claimed. Then will He restore to His servants the children that have been taken from them by death (*Prophets and Kings*, p. 239).

Today, if your faith begins to waver, remember the story of this humble woman. Like the noble Shunamite woman, remind God of His Word. Recall His promises of old, hold on by faith, believe that He will fulfill that which He has promised, and know that in Jesus "all is well."

Conversation

"Jesus looked at them and said to them, 'With men this is impossible, but with God all things are possible'" (Matthew 19:26).

"Now faith is the substance of things hoped for, the evidence of things not seen" (Hebrews 11:1).

"Jesus said to her, 'I am the resurrection and the life. He who believes in Me, though he may die he shall live'" (John 11:25).

Lessons I Learned:

(Reflect on opportunities for self-improvement.)

Personal Goal for Today:

(Identify one goal based on the reading.)

Today's Targets:

1.
2.
3.

(List three practical steps to help you reach your goal.)

Today I am thankful for:

(Write a short prayer of thanks to God for the blessings He has brought to you.)

A Faithful Witness

Colleen Townsley

"God has not given us a spirit of fear, but of power and of love and of a sound mind. Therefore do not be ashamed of the testimony of our Lord, nor of me His prisoner, but share with me in the sufferings for the gospel according to the power of God." —2 Timothy 1:7, 8

Have you ever felt so trapped by your circumstances that you didn't believe you were able to witness for God?

She awoke in the middle of the night to the sounds of family members screaming. At first she thought she was having a nightmare, but then her door was kicked in and an angry man pulled her from her bed, yelling at her in a foreign language. She cried out, "Daddy! Daddy! Help me!"—but there was no answer. As she was being carried out of her house, she saw bodies lying on the floor. *Were they dead?* "Mommy! Mommy! Wake up!"

Outside she heard more screams and, amid the chaos, saw playmates and neighbors being carried away as well. She was terrified, confused, so she did the only thing she knew to do in times of trouble; she prayed to God—*Lord, I don't know what is happening. I'm so scared. Please be with me. I know You are the King of kings, and even though I don't understand why this is happening, I will trust You.*

When she arrived at her new home and found she was in a land of idolatry, she vowed to stay faithful to the God of Israel, as her parents had always taught her. Her master, Naaman, was a commander in the king's army and was a mighty man of valor. She praised the Lord that he and his wife were kind and treated her well. Even though she was young, she understood that she was a slave and was considered part of the spoils of war; however, her faith was strong and she was able to find joy and satisfaction in honoring God through her thoughts, words, and deeds.

Her attitude was one of humility and cheerfulness, and she tried to uplift others henever she could. Because of this, she earned the respect and admiration of her master's ife, who was impressed by the resolve of the young child.

As the girl grew in favor with her mistress, she must have also gained her trust and onfidence—for she eventually learned that her master had leprosy, and she was bold enough tell them about Elisha, the prophet. "If only my master were with the prophet who is in amaria! For he would heal him of his leprosy" (2 Kings 5:3).

Now, for a mighty man of valor and a commander in the king's army to take the word of small slave girl to heart, he must have considered her trustworthy. One might suggest he was esperate, but keep in mind that Naaman went to his king and asked for permission—based n the counsel of a slave girl—to seek out Elisha, a prophet from the land of his enemy. As esperate as Naaman may have been, it would have to take enormous faith to go before he king with such a request. He must have believed there was substance in the faith of the ttle slave.

Naaman sought out Elisha, but when he arrived, something distressing happened. "Elisha ent a messenger to him, saying, 'Go and wash in the Jordan seven times, and your flesh shall e restored to you, and you shall be clean'" (2 Kings 5:10). Naaman was furious; he thought e'd been had! Wash in the filthy Jordan River seven times? But his servants convinced him o give it a try, and upon rising out of the water for the seventh time, his skin was like that of little child. It was a miracle! Imagine the impact it had on the servants with Naaman, the oldiers under his command, and his household.

The Lord used the weakest of the weak—the lowest of the low—to bring about niraculous healing for this man. A poor little slave girl, who could have succumbed to lepression and given up on the Lord entirely, instead chose to trust the Lord and follow Him vhatever the cost. She chose to remember the Scripture, "Though He slay me, yet will I trust Iim" (Job 13:15).

But how was such a young child able to do this? A recent study outlines some haracteristics that make it more likely that kids will do well in adverse situations. Two of he most important factors are the support of a caring and stable adult, and "the supportive ontext of affirming faith."[3]

The little slave girl had parents who loved and supported her and taught her about the God of the universe. She was instructed in the Scriptures from the time she was a babe on her nother's knee. Her family taught her by example—by living out their faith.

The conduct of the captive maid, the way that she bore herself in that heathen home, is a strong witness to the power of early home training. There is no higher trust than that committed to fathers and mothers in the care and training of their children. Parents have to do with the very foundations of habit and character. By their example and teaching the future of their children is largely decided (*Prophets and Kings*, p. 245).

Today, our busy lifestyles, financial troubles, dead-end jobs, lack of education—the list is endless—can make us feel enslaved and unable to answer the call to "let your light so shine before men" (Matthew 5:16). But we can still have a powerful influence on others through the same faith as that of the little slave girl. Regardless of our circumstances, there are always opportunities to witness through our attitudes and actions. God, our Father, provides the most stable, caring, and supportive relationship we can have. And combined with an affirming faith in His Word, we can triumph in reaching others for His glory.

Conversation

"Walk in wisdom toward those who are outside, redeeming the time. Let your speech always be with grace, seasoned with salt, that you may know how you ought to answer each one" (Colossians 4:5, 6).

"He said to me, 'My grace is sufficient for you, for My strength is made perfect in weakness.' Therefore most gladly I will rather boast in my infirmities, that the power of Christ may rest upon me" (2 Corinthians 12:9).

"And we know that all things work together for good to those who love God, to those who are the called according to His purpose" (Romans 8:28).

---

3 https://www.gse.harvard.edu/news/uk/15/03/science-resilience

Lessons I Learned:

(Reflect on opportunities for self-improvement.)

Personal Goal for Today:

(Identify one goal based on the reading.)

Today's Targets:

1.

2.

3.

(List three practical steps to help you reach your goal.)

Today I am thankful for:

(Write a short prayer of thanks to God for the blessings He has brought to you.)

For Such a Time as This

Carissa McSherry

"Greater love has no one than this, than to lay down one's life for his friends."—John 15:13

Have you ever given up something you truly loved in order to help a friend–or maybe even an enemy?

Fear, doubt, and desperation all clamored at once for her attention. Questions swirled like a hurricane through her mind as she considered her probable fate.

After all, the king wasn't known for his leniency. Wasn't his former wife punished just a few years back for an act less daring than this? But in her heart, Esther knew that death at the hand of her husband would be far less painful than surviving unscathed as she witnessed the brutal destruction of her people.

With her head held high and her mind made up, Esther walked forward with unfaltering steps into the audience chamber of her king.

From a young age, Esther had deeply loved Mordecai. When she was left orphaned after the death of her parents, Mordecai was the one who stepped in to raise her like a child of his own. She trusted his counsel. She yearned to be near him in his time of suffering—as he mourned the imminent death of his people and possibly struggled with guilt, knowing that it was because of Haman's hatred for him that the entire Jewish nation in Persia would soon be slain.

Esther waited anxiously for the messenger's report. It was far too dangerous for her to blow her cover and approach Mordecai herself. In fact, Mordecai was the one who had sworn her to secrecy about her true identity in the first place.

Finally, Mordecai's message was delivered: "Do not think in your heart that you will escape in the king's palace any more than all the other Jews. For if you remain completely ent at this time, relief and deliverance will arise for the Jews from another place, but you d your father's house will perish. Yet who knows whether you have come to the kingdom for ch a time as this?" (Esther 4:13, 14).

The words pierced Esther's heart. She wasn't just another young woman among many the king's harem; her life had a purpose! Could it be that the God of heaven had placed her the palace for such a time as this? Esther replied, "Go, gather all the Jews who are present Shushan, and fast for me; neither eat nor drink for three days, night or day. My maids and I ill fast likewise. And so I will go to the king, which is against the law; and if I perish, I perish!" sther 4:16).

Even at the risk of her life, Esther would stand faithful on behalf of her people.

A similar testimony is seen in the life of Moses. After forty days of solitude in the mount ith God, Moses' dialogue with God came to an abrupt halt at the sound of noise in the camp low. Not the noise of war, as was presumed, but of the worship of a golden calf.

With every step, his indignation burned more fiercely. Taking the golden calf away om the startled worshipers, Moses burnt their god before them, ground it into powder, and rced them to drink the remnants of that which they had once worshiped. "What did this ople do to you that you have brought so great a sin upon them?" Moses demanded of Aaron xodus 32:21). The excuses of the religious leader satisfied neither Moses nor God. Three ousand men died in their rebellion on that heartbreaking day.

Moses, seeing that atonement must still be made for the remainder of the camp, t off again into the presence of God. With a heart of humility, Moses pled, "These people ave committed a great sin, and have made for themselves a god of gold! Yet now, if You ill forgive their sin—but if not, I pray, blot me out of Your book which You have written" xodus 32:31, 32).

Though the guilt did not rest upon his shoulders, Moses was willing to accept the blame nd to lay down his life with the people rather than to live in the Promised Land without them.

These snapshots from the lives of Esther and Moses were written to point us to a greater ory still, to the Son of God. Jesus assured the listening crowd, "I have come that they may ave life, and that they may have it more abundantly. I am the good shepherd. The good epherd gives His life for the sheep" (John 10:10, 11).

As in the stories recorded before, Jesus did not have to accept the guilt of fallen man. He ould have dwelt in peace in the glories of heaven without ever feeling the pain of separation om His Father and the cruel torments of sinful man. But to Jesus, not even His life was too reat a sacrifice for the salvation of His children.

As one author wrote, "Jesus did not consider heaven a place to be desired while we wer lost. He left the heavenly courts for a life of reproach and insult, and a death of shame. He wh was rich in heaven's priceless treasure became poor, that through His poverty we might be ric We are to follow in the path He trod" (*Ministry of Healing*, p. 105).

Jesus gave us the ultimate example of self-sacrificing love—a love that desires the salvation of others above our own desires, our own needs, or even our own lives.

Hudson Taylor, a faithful pioneer missionary to China, was known for his fervent prayers on behalf of the Chinese people. He was once heard praying, "God, give me China or I die!" Because he gave his all to the souls in China, God trusted the souls in China to him.

Today, we may not be called to forfeit our lives on behalf of another, but perhaps today God is calling us to lay down our pride, our passions, and our self-serving ways for the greater good of those around us. Or maybe He is calling us to earnestly pray, "God, give me this neighborhood! God, give me my coworkers! God, give me my family! Lest I die."

May our lives be a living sacrifice, willingly laid down for His lost sheep, as we answer th call He has given us "for such a time as this."

"He was wounded for our transgressions, he was bruised for our iniquities; the chastisement for our peace was upon Him, and by His stripes we are healed. All we like sheep have gone astray; we have turned, every one, to his own way; and the LORD has laid on Him the iniquity of us all" (Isaiah 53:5, 6).

"He who does not take his cross and follow after Me is not worthy of Me" (Matthew 10:38).

"Whoever desires to save his life will lose it, but whoever loses his life for My sake will find it" (Matthew 16:25).

essons I Learned:

(eflect on opportunities for self-improvement.)

ersonal Goal for Today:

(dentify one goal based on the reading.)

oday's Targets:

-
-
-

(List three practical steps to help you reach your goal.)

oday I am thankful for:

(Write a short prayer of thanks to God for the blessings He has brought to you.)

A Woman after God's Own Heart

Michelle Kiss

> *"Charm is deceitful and beauty is passing, but a woman who fears the LORD, she shall be praised." —Proverbs 31:30*

Have you ever wondered how you can be a woman after God's own heart?

The woman described in Proverbs 31 is not a specific woman that we find in the Bible. However, the characteristics of this strong, God-fearing woman are reflected in the stories of the well-known godly women we find in the pages of the Scriptures. This passage also describes the kind of woman that God wants us to be. Whether married, unmarried, with children or without, the characteristics outlined in Proverbs 31 describe a woman after God's own heart.

In Proverbs 31:30 we read, "Charm is deceitful and beauty is passing, but a woman who fears the LORD, she shall be praised." Of course, this verse is not saying that beauty is a sin. After all, God created beautiful things. What it means is that beauty is short-lived or temporary—it's something that will not last. As we grow older, beauty will begin to fade, and no matter how we may try and fight it, we will ultimately lose the battle.

Every day, we are visually bombarded with messages telling us how we should look. From magazines to electronic media, we are continuously inundated with messages telling us that to be accepted, we have to dress in the latest fashions, have the newest hairstyles, and practically starve ourselves thin. Society tells us that our appearance and level of success in the home and in the workplace is what makes us valuable. Pressure is placed upon us as women to be the perfect image of what "man" wants. But this is not what God wants. God tells us that what's on the inside—the beautiful character created through a daily walk with Him—is what is of the greatest value. "Do not let your adornment be merely outward . . . rather let it be the hidden person of the heart, with the incorruptible beauty of a gentle and quiet spirit, which is very precious in the sight of God" (1 Peter 3:3, 4).

What God values and praises is a "woman who fears the LORD." So what does it mean to ear the Lord? It means that we honor by obedience, respect, and revere Him. People may fear a vorldly king because they're afraid of what he may do to them. But if he is a kind and just king, heir negative fear will turn into respect and awe.

This is the same in our relationship with God; when we take time with Him daily, we vill get to know Him for the kind and loving God that He really is. And we will also be taking teps that will lead us on the path to becoming the women God wants us to be. When we nderstand God's love for us, and His gift of salvation, it will show in the way we live our ives; our actions will begin to reflect that we have been with God. The Proverbs 31 woman xemplifies the characteristics of a godly woman, and this is what is so beautiful about her.

She is also a woman of faith who seeks wisdom in everything she does. She is kind-earted and careful in the words she speaks to and about others. Proverbs 31:26 says, "She opens her mouth with wisdom, and on her tongue is the law of kindness." It is evident that he is very committed to her marriage and her family. Her husband knows he can fully trust er with his heart and everything that's under her care (verses 11, 12). She is well respected nd loved by her family and watches over her household (verses 27, 28). She is virtuous, rustworthy, hardworking, and an excellent steward of time and money. She is selfless, caring, ospitable, and looks after the needy (verse 20). And she knows the importance of caring for erself and her health (verse 17).

Even though the Proverbs 31 woman was not an actual person, we may look at the haracteristics that describe this "perfect" woman and think to ourselves, *How can I ever come lose? There's just no way!* But God is not looking for perfection; He is looking for a heart that is villing to grow and to serve and follow Him. And the more time we spend with Him, the more ve will become like Him and reflect His image.

"A long time ago, a few ladies met to read Scripture and make the writings the subject of conversation. While reading the third chapter of Malachi, they came upon a remarkable expression in the third verse, 'And He shall sit as a refiner and purifier of silver.' One lady proposed to visit a silversmith and report to them what he said on the subject. As she watched the silversmith, he held a piece of silver over the fire and let it heat up. He explained how when efining silver, one needed to hold the silver in the middle of the fire where the flames were the hottest so to burn away all the impurities.

'But sir,' she said, 'do you sit while the work of refining is going on?'

'Oh, yes, madam,' replied the silversmith, 'I must sit with my eyes steadily fixed on the furnace, for if the time necessary for refining be exceeded in the slightest degree, the silver would be destroyed.' The woman was silent for a moment. Then she asked the silversmith, 'How do you know when the silver is fully refined?' He answered, 'Oh, that's the easy part—when I see my image reflected in it.'" (Author unknown) [4]

This story of the silversmith beautifully illustrates the work God does in our lives. In and of ourselves, we cannot reach any level of "perfection." As the Bible says in John 15:5, "I am the vine, you are the branches. He who abides in Me, and I in him, bears much fruit; for without Me you can do nothing." So wherever we are in our journey with Christ, let's remember that God is in control. Let's daily seek Him and put our trust in Him. He is the Silversmith that purifies, polishes, and refines, and He will make us into the women He wants us to be—until the impurities in our characters are removed and we begin to reflect the image of Christ.

Conversation

"The wise woman builds her house, but the foolish pulls it down with her hands" (Proverbs 14:1).

"And whatever you do, do it heartily, as to the Lord and not to men, knowing that from the Lord you will receive the reward of inheritance; for you serve the Lord Christ" (Colossians 3:23, 24).

"And do not be conformed to this world, but be transformed by the renewing of your mind, that you may prove what is that good and acceptable and perfect will of God" (Romans 12:2).

---

4 http://www.clarion-call.org/extras/malachi.htm.

Lessons I Learned:

(Reflect on opportunities for self-improvement.)

Personal Goal for Today:

(Identify one goal based on the reading.)

Today's Targets:

1.
2.
3.

(List three practical steps to help you reach your goal.)

Today I am thankful for:

(Write a short prayer of thanks to God for the blessings He has brought to you.)

Taking God at His Word

Jena Kilmer

"Having been born again, not of corruptible seed but incorruptible, through the Word of God which lives and abides forever."—1 Peter 1:23

Have you ever felt the word "faith" was just another empty, spiritual word that makes no difference in your daily life?

Imagine this situation: You have met the man of your dreams. You seem to be perfect for one another; you even think that God played a role in bringing the two of you together. You have since been sweating through the tough work involved in planning a wedding. It's exhausting, but you're grateful that all the pieces seem to be falling into place. The big day that you have dreamed about for years is coming. But then something strange happens. You get a totally unexpected message: You are pregnant! You know you haven't been unfaithful. What would your husband-to-be say? How would you explain it all?

Even though wedding traditions were different then, Mary, the mother of our Savior, must have experienced these feelings. As she was planning to get married to Joseph, an angel visited her, bringing her the most unexpected and unlikely message she could have imagined. Could she really become a mother as a virgin? How could that be? What would she say to Joseph? She must have had thousands of thoughts in her head. *Me, highly favored and blessed among women?* (Luke 1:28). *My son will be great and be called the Son of the Highest—to reign over the house of Jacob forever?* (Luke 1:32, 33). *Will my son really be the Messiah we have long hoped for?*

Do you think Mary wondered, *Why me—among so many other women?* It's a good question! Something made it possible for God to entrust her with one of the greatest works a human has ever been given—to give birth to and care for the Creator! Something made it possible for God to do the impossible in her life.

What was that something? And could it be that God is longing to see more of that something in our lives today?

God has given many unlikely and seemingly impossible messages to many people throughout history. Noah was warned about a worldwide Flood and told to build an ark. Did he tell God how much work it would take to build an ark that size—or did he just build the ark? God told Moses that the Israelites would be given the Promised Land, yet they sent in spies. Seeing all the giants inhabiting the land didn't really help them respond in faith to God's Word. Abraham and Sarah were told by God that they would become parents long after it is typically possible for women to have babies. I am sure you remember how they responded to God's Word. Instead of a trusting "Let it be to me according to your word" (Luke 1:38), there was laughter, unbelief—letting God know it was impossible.

The stories are many, and we clearly see that there are two different ways of responding to God's Word. How I choose to respond to the Word of God seems to determine whether the creative power of the Word can be unfolded or not.

Some words from the book *Education* by Ellen G. White have fascinated me many times and awakened my respect for the Bible. On page 126, she says,

> The creative energy that called the worlds into existence is in the word of God. This word imparts power; it begets life. Every command is a promise; accepted by the will, received into the soul, it brings with it the life of the Infinite One. It transforms the nature and re-creates the soul in the image of God. The life thus imparted is in like manner sustained. "By every word that proceedeth out of the mouth of God" (Matthew 4:4) shall man live.

Although the words we speak can bring huge consequences, it is different when God speaks. God can create from nothing just by calling it forth with his own mouth (Psalm 33:9; Genesis 1). Yet my response to God's Word matters. I can either close the door of heaven's storehouse or I can receive the creative power that, even today, is hidden in the Word of God.

When fighting through one of the most fear–inducing and difficult issues in my own life, I felt God had given me a special promise to hang on to. Psalm 138:8 says: "The Lord will perfect that which concerns me." There is nothing more precious in life than the experience of knowing that God is near and speaks to me in my life situation. Faith is to hold on to what we do not see, as if it were in plain sight (Hebrews 11:1–3). I realized how hard it was for me to believe the promise that God had given me. I would freely believe when peacefully reading my Bible, but when the stress of daily life came, I cannot tell you that I had perfect peace all the time. I was tempted to give in to fear and discouragement; many times I did. With feelings of hopelessness and fear filling my heart, I slowly and gradually learned that I still had the power to choose what I allowed my mouth to speak. Often with tears in my eyes, the words from the psalmist were spoken: "The Lord will perfect that which concerns me."

The struggle is one that comes and goes, but I know He works in each and every situation. I can focus my eyes on Him whose word has creative power, and say with Mary, "Let it be to me according to your word" (Luke 1:38).

"The word of the Lord is proven; He is a shield to all who trust in Him" (Psalm 18:30).

"He who heeds the word wisely will find good, and whoever trusts in the Lord, happy is he" (Proverbs 16:20).

"This is my comfort in my affliction, for Your word has given me life" (Psalm 119:50).

"Those who fear You will be glad when they see me, because I have hoped in Your word" (Psalm 119:74).

Lessons I Learned:

(Reflect on opportunities for self-improvement.)

Personal Goal for Today:

(Identify one goal based on the reading.)

Today's Targets:

1.

2.

3.

(List three practical steps to help you reach your goal.)

Today I am thankful for:

(Write a short prayer of thanks to God for the blessings He has brought to you.)

Persistent Prayer

Laurie Lyon

"Rejoicing in hope, patient in tribulation, continuing steadfastly in prayer."—Romans 12:12

Have you ever prayed for something to happen and wondered if your prayers were heard?

After the tragic death of her husband, CarolMarie felt that she had lost everything. Not only had she lost her best friend, but her business had recently failed, and she was drowning in million-dollar debt. It wasn't long before her home and vehicles were gone. The only income she had was the $277 a month her husband had left to her. It was a daunting situation, and she was tempted to give up.

Instead, she turned to persistent prayer.

Within two years, CarolMarie began volunteering at a ministry center for widows. When a chaplain asked her to teach a grief class, she hesitated. Still reeling from her own grief, she wondered how she could manage it. But after praying about it, she decided to give it a try.

And as she continued to pray and serve the Lord by spreading hope and comfort to others, she was blessed. Although she didn't advertise her needs, people provided donations to support her and her ministry. In time, she paid off her debt. And as she shared gifts with various ministries and individuals, her blessings were multiplied.

CarolMarie's ministry teaches hurting people to look to God as their Source of hope, their support, and the One who can answer their deepest prayers.[5]

In a similar way, the prophetess Anna allowed God to take her heart-rending situation and turn it into a blessing for her and for others. Luke is the only Gospel writer to record her experience, and there are few details in his account. But there is enough to intrigue us with her unusual story and to inspire us with her overwhelmingly positive response to the trials that she faced.

Widowed at a very young age—only seven years into her marriage—she must have been pressed by friends and relatives to remarry. Here she was, likely in her early twenties, with a traumatized heart but a full life ahead of her. Surely she could find another husband and start over again. But despite their probable prodding, Anna chose a different path.

Instead of giving in to her distressing circumstances, Anna turned her eyes heavenward and became a woman of persistent prayer. Throughout her life, she chose to continue thanking God for His rich blessings, pleading for the arrival of the Promised One, and dedicating her life to serving Him. It must have been heart-wrenching for her to see her people drifting further and further away from the Lord, but she continued to pray earnestly for them.

The Bible tells us that at the time when Jesus was brought to the temple in Jerusalem for dedication to God, Anna "did not depart from the temple, but served God with fastings and prayers night and day" (Luke 2:37). Though the Scriptures do not explain this arrangement in detail, many scholars believe that she lived in or near the temple, and that she may have been given living quarters because of her position as a prophetess. Although many of the priests of that time had wandered away from the Lord, there were those who were faithful to Him and could have provided for this servant of God.

The Bible also says that Anna was "a widow of about eighty-four years" (verses 37). Here, opinions differ, since the verse can be interpreted in different ways. Perhaps she was 84 years old, but many believe that because the Bible highlights the fact that she was "of a great age" (verse 36), she had been widowed 84 years earlier. So Anna could have been in the neighborhood of 105 years of age! And here she was, still fasting and praying, eagerly anticipating the arrival of the promised Messiah and the salvation of her people.

Although Anna's life was not an easy one, all of her faith was in the Lord, and He did not disappoint. Besides providing for her physical needs, God rewarded her faithful prayers. He honored this woman who honored Him by allowing her to meet her Savior in person. Perhaps with dimming eyesight, she would nevertheless clearly see the Messiah in whom she had put her hope for so many years.

As Simeon was holding Jesus and testifying to the light He would bring, Anna joined them. "Coming in that instant she gave thanks to the Lord" (Luke 2:38).

Because she had persisted in prayer and had built a deep relationship with the Lord, her recognition of Him was immediate. This was her Savior, come to bring hope and salvation to His people!

This was the moment she had been waiting for all her life, the culmination of all of her hopes and a lifetime of relentless prayers, and she was ecstatic as she confirmed the testimony of Simeon. "As Simeon spoke, her face lighted up with the glory of God, and she poured out her heartfelt thanks that she had been permitted to behold Christ the Lord" (*The Desire of Ages*, p. 55).

As Anna looked into the beautiful face of her Redeemer, all the sufferings of her life faded into insignificance. Scripture records that Anna then "spoke of Him to all those who looked for redemption in Jerusalem" (verse 38). With overflowing joy, she spread the news that was too wonderful to keep to herself. The persistent prayers of all the faithful had come to fruition. The Savior of the world had arrived!

What trials do you face today? Problems with finances, health, or relationships? The loss of someone dear? Struggles with temptation? Loved ones with no interest in the things of God? Our world overflows with discouraging events and situations that can sap our hope. The solution is to persist in prayer, knowing that the Lord hears your praises as well as your cries for help. "He hears the prayer of the righteous" (Proverbs 15:29).

Like the faithful Anna, seek the Savior through a solid prayer life. Persist in pouring out your heart to Jesus. He offers you security, purpose, and the ultimate fulfillment of your hopes and prayers. You will find all you need or could ever want in knowing and serving Him. And one day soon you, too, can look joyfully into the beautiful face of your Redeemer.

"Praying always with all prayer and supplication in the Spirit, being watchful to this end with all perseverance and supplication for all the saints" (Ephesians 6:18).

"Evening and morning and at noon I will pray, and cry aloud, and He shall hear my voice" (Psalm 55:17).

"Continue earnestly in prayer, being vigilant in it with thanksgiving" (Colossians 4:2).

---

5 http://archive.knoxnews.com/entertainment/family/widow-finds-healing-in-helping-others-ep-361181513-357212081.html

Lessons I Learned:

(Reflect on opportunities for self-improvement.)

Personal Goal for Today:

(Identify one goal based on the reading.)

Today's Targets:

1.
2.
3.

(List three practical steps to help you reach your goal.)

Today I am thankful for:

(Write a short prayer of thanks to God for the blessings He has brought to you.)

Day 22

The Widow of Nain

Dianne Cossentine

"When He came near the gate of the city, behold, a dead man was being carried out, the only son of his mother; and she was a widow. And a large crowd from the city was with her. When the Lord saw her, He had compassion on her and said to her, 'Do not weep.'" —*Luke 7:12, 13*

Has your life ever come screeching to a halt–and it felt like there was no way forward?

She was now utterly destitute. Her husband had died and left her alone with their child. Fortunately, it was a son, old enough to work and support her. At that time women could not own property, and they could not hold a paying job. Now that her son was dead, she was left entirely at the mercy of others to support her.

Funerals were well attended in her day. It was part of the culture to show up and grieve loudly at funeral processions. But how many of those people would stick around to support her afterward? Did she look apprehensively at the faces around her, wondering who, if anyone, would help her the next day, the next month, the next year?

They walked along the road to the cemetery with many women out in front wailing loudly. Her son was in an open casket, carried by men who took turns to honor the family. The mother walked numbly next to the casket, lost in her grief.

Suddenly, the procession stopped—a man was blocking the way. She had no idea who this person was; but he walked up and stopped before her. Jesus looked like any other man. The stranger spoke; looking tenderly at her, He said, "Don't cry."

Don't cry? She probably was shocked at the stranger's audacity. He could have no idea of what she had just gone through and that she was now a destitute widow. But then she looked into His eyes and began to realize the depth of His compassion.

In Jesus' day, it was highly unusual for a Jewish man to touch a dead body, which required seven days of cleansing afterward. But Jesus wasn't afraid to get dirty in His ministry to others. Without hesitation, He reached over and laid His hand on the women's son and said, "Young man, I say to you, arise!" (Luke 7:14).

Instantly, the son sat up and started talking. This was no gradual healing. He was immediately alive, awake, and alert. What do you suppose the son said? Did he look around him, confused that he was sitting in an open casket surrounded by throngs of stunned people staring at him? "Wh-what's going on?" The pallbearers set the casket down, and Jesus helped the young man to stand up and presented him to his mother. His mother must have been overwhelmed with emotion, crying and stammering thanks to Jesus and hugging her son with joy.

Notice that Jesus didn't ask the son to follow Him as He had so many others. He knew where the son was most needed. Jesus knew what His own mother was soon going to experience, and He hoped His followers would care for her compassionately.

This young man is the first of three people that Jesus is known to have resurrected. No one had raised the dead since Elisha, so no one would have thought of asking Him to resurrect anyone. The mother didn't ask Jesus to resurrect her son. It is possible that she had never even heard of Him or the people He had healed. There is nothing she could have done to earn this miracle. Jesus saw her need and ministered to her without even being asked. God doesn't just love the world as a whole, He loves us and cares for us as individuals. We don't have to convince Him to love us or beg Him to help us. "The Lord is gracious and full of compassion" (Psalm 111:4).

Are our own actions motivated by compassion, or are we kind only because we think we are supposed to do nice things? Do we do kind acts only if someone can see us and we can receive praise for it? Do we do things quietly, or are we sure to tell others how awesome we are? How do we show compassion in our lives?

Use the Golden Rule and treat others as you like to be treated. When you receive emails and phone calls at work or at home, reply to them right away—as promptly as you like to receive responses. When you are in line at the grocery store with a cart full of food and the person behind you has only a couple of items, let them go ahead of you. Every day presents opportunities to show compassion to others; little kindnesses can go a long way toward encouraging someone.

Sometimes life seems to screech to a halt and we are thrown into a desperate time. It can feel like there is no way out. To the widow in the funeral procession, life seemed hopeless, and even more frustrating when Jesus halted the procession. But in that halt came healing, and a good change in life. Our lives have different seasons—relationships change, jobs change, housing changes—and it can be deeply distressing. Pray that you will know God's will for your life. Trust that He has good things waiting for you. "Rest in the Lord, and wait patiently for Him" (Psalm 37:7). God has compassion for everyone and wants the best for us. When Jesus stops your life progress, pause and let Him work.

"The Lord is good to all, and His tender mercies are over all His works" (Psalm 145:8, 9).

"All of you be of one mind, having compassion for one another; love as brothers, be tenderhearted, be courteous; not returning evil for evil or reviling for reviling, but on the contrary blessing, knowing that you were called to this" (1 Peter 3:8, 9).

"A father of the fatherless, a defender of widows, is God in His holy habitation" (Psalm 68:5).

Daily Reflection

Lessons I Learned:

(Reflect on opportunities for self-improvement.)

Personal Goal for Today:

(Identify one goal based on the reading.)

Today's Targets:

1.
2.
3.

(List three practical steps to help you reach your goal.)

Today I am thankful for:

(Write a short prayer of thanks to God for the blessings He has brought to you.)

Bringing a Village

Marsha Schick

"As the body without the spirit is dead, so faith without works is dead also." —James 2:26

Have you ever had an experience with Christ that inspired you to tell everyone you know about it?

In the Samaritan city of Sychar stood a very special well. There the people would draw water for their daily drinking, cooking, and washing. But as ordinary as this well may have seemed, it held great significance to the residents of Samaria. The ancestors of these people had been Jews. A disunion caused by captivity led to mixed marriages and idolatry, causing a rift between the full-blooded Jews and the pagan-influenced Samaritans, but the Samaritans clung to their heritage as descendants of the patriarch Jacob.

Many Jews preferred to walk around Samaria on their way to Jerusalem, adding countless hours to their journey because of their hatred for Samaritans. But Jesus walked right into Samaria with His disciples—on a mission the disciples did not yet understand. Leaving Him at the well, the disciples went into the city to buy food.

As Jesus rested by the well, a woman came to draw water in the heat of the day. "Give me a drink," He asked gently. The woman was taken aback. She was aware of the stigma the Jews had placed on the Samaritans and was amazed that this Jew would speak to her. She said, "How is it that You, being a Jew, ask a drink from me, a Samaritan woman?" (John 4:9).

Jesus responded, "If you knew the gift of God, and who it is who says to you, 'Give Me a drink,' you would have asked Him, and He would have given you living water" (verse 10). God wants us to ask Him to fill our needs in accordance with His will.

The woman pointed out that the well was deep and Jesus had nothing with which to draw water. "Where then do You get that living water? Are you greater than our father

Jacob, who gave us the well, and drank from it himself, as well as his sons and his livestock?" (vv. 11, 12). The woman lost no opportunity to boast of her heritage—and the pointed question could be seen as an invitation for a religious debate—but Jesus was focused on a greater need.

"Whoever drinks of this water will thirst again, but whoever drinks of the water that I shall give him will never thirst. But the water that I shall give him will become in him a fountain of water springing up into everlasting life" (vv. 13, 14).

It was an offer she could not turn down. "Sir, give me this water, that I may not thirst, nor come here to draw" (v. 15). Although the woman did not immediately understand, Jesus was using the context in which He found her to share the gospel. He was pointing her to the Holy Spirit who first convicts us of sin and then points us to Christ.

At another time, Jesus said, "If anyone thirsts, let him come to Me and drink. He who believes in Me, as the Scripture has said, out of his heart will flow rivers of living water" (John 7:37, 38). The passage goes on to say that He was talking about the Holy Spirit. The Holy Spirit helps us to understand God's Word, guides us through life's perplexities and helps us overcome sin. He fills us with a supernatural joy even in the midst of the most trying circumstances.

Jesus asked the woman to go call her husband and return. This would seem out of place without understanding the work of the Holy Spirit. "When [the Holy Spirit] has come, He will convict the world of sin, and of righteousness, and of judgment" (John 16:8). It's this conviction of sin that leads us to see our need for Christ.

The woman answered that she had no husband. Jesus then said, "You have well said, 'I have no husband,' for you have had five husbands, and the one whom you now have is not your husband; in that you spoke truly" (John 4:17, 18). Jesus pointed out her sin, not to shame her but to liberate her from her past. We cannot rid the sin from our lives without first recognizing the hold it has on us, and this is what Jesus was helping her to do.

The woman was beginning to see that there was something extraordinary about this Jew who was speaking to her with such tender care. She suspected He might be a prophet, but she didn't yet recognize Him as the Son of God. Later in their conversation, the woman said, "I know that Messiah is coming. . . . When He comes, He will tell us all things" (v. 25). And Jesus assured her that He was the Messiah.

In her excitement, the woman left her water pot and ran into the city and told others she had met a man who told her everything she had ever done. "Could this be the Christ?" (v. 29), she asked. The residents then hurried out to see for themselves.

Once she had met Jesus, this woman's thirst for physical water dissipated as her thirst for spiritual water had begun to grow! This unnamed Samaritan woman had complete faith that she had met her Savior, and her enthusiasm played a major role in leading virtually an entire city to Christ after she had first received Him. Because of her testimony, many of those people became believers.

Today, do you recognize Jesus as the Messiah? Are you receiving living water from Him? If so, how can you share Him with those in your sphere of influence? How can you point others to the only One who can give them real hope and purpose for their lives?

"It is done! I am the Alpha and the Omega, the Beginning and the End. I will give of the fountain of the water of life freely to him who thirsts" (Revelation 21:6).

"By this My Father is glorified, that you bear much fruit; so you will be My disciples" (John 15:8).

"Blessed be the God and Father of our Lord Jesus Christ, who according to His abundant mercy has begotten us again to a living hope through the resurrection of Jesus Christ from the dead, to an inheritance incorruptible and undefiled and that does not fade away, reserved in heaven for you, who are kept by the power of God through faith for salvation ready to be revealed in the last time" (1 Peter 1:3–5).

Lessons I Learned:

(Reflect on opportunities for self-improvement.)

Personal Goal for Today:

(Identify one goal based on the reading.)

Today's Targets:

1.
2.
3.

(List three practical steps to help you reach your goal.)

Today I am thankful for:

(Write a short prayer of thanks to God for the blessings He has brought to you.)

Day 24

The Touch of Faith

Carissa McSherry

"Daughter, be of good cheer; your faith has made you well. Go in peace." —Luke 8:48

Do you ever feel as though your prayers are not heard? What could be keeping you from receiving the healing that your heart so desperately craves?

Time was of the essence. Every moment that passed was excruciating to the father of a dying twelve-year-old girl. But the pressure of the crowd and the pleas of a desperate father were not enough to distract Christ from the need at hand.

A woman. Depressed, discouraged, penniless, and lonely after twelve long years of illness She had spent all that she possessed in a vain attempt to receive healing. Her clammy, pale skin testified of her daily weakening condition. She had all but resigned herself to death when news reached her ears of a great Healer—of a man, traveling throughout her region, who had healed whole cities! Hope once again sprang into her heart.

Rising early in the morning, she made an exhausting journey to the center of town, not far from home, hoping to catch a glimpse of Jesus. But soon, she recognized that she was not alone. Hundreds of others had gathered with this same idea in mind. How could she possibly see Jesus?

The growing noise of the crowd indicated that Jesus was drawing near. Though nearly cast aside by the pushing of the excited mob, she leapt forward in desperation and grasped the robe of the Savior. Instantly, she knew that she had been healed.

"Who touched Me?" Jesus stopped to ask. Known for His perceptive questions, this inquiry must have surprised the listening disciples. "Master, the multitudes throng and press You, and You say, 'Who touched Me?' But Jesus said, 'Somebody touched Me, for I perceived power going out from Me' " (Luke 8:45, 46).

At this, the woman came trembling to His feet. Falling before Him, she declared that she indeed had touched His robe and that now she was healed. With calm assurance, Jesus soothed her trembling heart: "Daughter, be of good cheer; your faith has made you well" (Luke 8:48).

According to *The Ministry of Healing*, "Christ knew every thought of her mind, and He was making His way to where she stood. He realized her great need, and He was helping her to exercise faith" (p. 60). Similarly, when we seek after God in prayer, we can know—with certainty—that Christ is already moving toward us, helping us to exercise and grow in our faith.

You see, many people touched Jesus that day. A whole multitude pressed into His presence! But only one received healing—the one who reached forward in full dependence upon Him. The one who reached forward by faith.

Maybe you have grown up attending church. You actively participate every weekend, even attending prayer meeting. But you still leave feeling empty and distant from God. Could it be that like the multitude around Jesus, you are bumping into Him casually, but not truly grasping onto His robe in full dependence by faith? Because only then will we receive healing.

Like Jacob of old, this woman would not let Jesus go until He blessed her. Christ yearns for this same persistence today! God is yearning for children who do not carelessly approach His presence or throw a quick prayer heavenward, expecting it to meet the requirements, but who instead seek to press into His presence until their burdens have been lifted at the feet of Calvary. He is calling us to press into His presence today.

Or maybe you, like this woman with the issue of blood, feel as though God doesn't hear your cry. Maybe it feels as though your prayers hit the ceiling and vibrate back to you. If so, claim this promise as your own today:

> Amid the anthems of the celestial choir, God hears the cries of the weakest human being. We pour out our heart's desire in our closets, we breathe a prayer as we walk by the way, and our words reach the throne of the Monarch of the universe. They may be inaudible to any human ear, but they cannot die away into silence, nor can they be lost through the activities of business that are going on. Nothing can drown the soul's desire. It rises above the din of the street, above the confusion of the multitude, to the heavenly courts. It is God to whom we are speaking, and our prayer is heard (*Christ's Object Lessons*, p. 174).

Seventeen days had passed since the collapse of an eight-story building in Dhaka, Bangladesh. Over 1,000 people had died in this tragic disaster. No survivors had been found for days, and certainly no more were expected. Demolition vehicles had arrived to clean up what remained of the rubble. Out of the corner of her eye, one worker noticed a strange movement. Upon further investigation, she realized that it was a trapped woman! "Please save me," Reshma pled from beneath the rubble. Amazingly, seventeen days after the collapse, Reshma was rescued and went on to make a full recovery.[6] Though she feared her cries would go unnoticed, they had indeed been heard.

So also today, Jesus hears your prayer. He knows your heart's desire. Jesus is answering that cry and moving closer to you, offering His healing presence. Are you willing to reach out and grasp His robe by faith today?

"Let us not grow weary while doing good, for in due season we shall reap if we do not lose heart" (Galatians 6:9).

"Now this is the confidence that we have in Him, that if we ask anything according to His will, He hears us" (1 John 5:14).

"Ask, and it will be given to you; seek, and you will find; knock, and it will be opened to you" (Matthew 7:7).

---

6 http://www.bbc.com/news/world-asia-22477414#TWEET750806

Daily Reflection

Lessons I Learned:

(Reflect on opportunities for self-improvement.)

Personal Goal for Today:

(Identify one goal based on the reading.)

Today's Targets:

1.
2.
3.

(List three practical steps to help you reach your goal.)

Today I am thankful for:

(Write a short prayer of thanks to God for the blessings He has brought to you.)

Faith Rewarded

Cyndee Holmes

"God has not given us a spirit of fear, but of power and of love and of a sound mind." —2 Timothy 1:7

Have you ever felt ignored or dismissed? Or have you felt the pain of prejudice?

Elissa stopped to catch her breath.

She'd been rushing up the hill, driven by desperation and the last ounce of hope that, perhaps, she would finally find someone who could heal her daughter. Her heart pounded from the exertion, so she paused a moment to rest. She then looked back from where she had come. Across the valley, she could see the coastal cities of Tyre and Sidon sparkling in the spring sunshine. Yet the beauty of the scene did not match the conflicted feelings in Elissa's heart.

She thought of poor Chara, her tormented daughter, who was skin and bones now due to the violent seizures that frequently wracked her tiny body. Chara's life had been far from happy—afflicted with what all the experts were saying was demon possession. For years now she had sought a cure, going from shrine to shrine, making sacrifices and countless payments to sorcerers and priests. Hopes had been highest when they traveled to the grand temple in Sidon, dedicated to Eshmun, the Phoenician god of healing. Surely this powerful god, so famous in their region, could cure her daughter! But all those rituals and sacrifices had been for nothing. Chara continued to decline.

There was a Jewish settlement in Tyre, and Elissa had even consulted the rabbis there. But they had emphatically told her that their God, Yahweh, would only help the Jews—and certainly not a Canaanite like her. The prejudice in their eyes was evident, and when she walked away, she could see them rushing to a basin for ritual cleansing after having talked with a pagan woman.

Elissa's family, friends, and neighbors had finally concluded that she and Chara were ursed and began to shun them. It was thought by most that they must have committed ome heinous sin, and the gods could not be appeased. Elissa had never been one to be easily iscouraged, but now sadness, worry, and deep loneliness plagued her days.

However, when she visited the market the day before, she'd overheard someone talk bout a great teacher in Israel. The man had been traveling the countryside, sharing unusual tories and revolutionary ideas about God. It was said that he had healed hundreds—and ven cast out demons. Someone said that the man and his followers had recently left the egion of Galilee, heading into the hill country along the border of Syria. Elissa didn't wait to ear more. She ran home, arranged for a servant to stay with Chara, and began her trek into he hill country to plead with this man on behalf of her daughter.

Elissa then turned to continue her trip up the hill. As she rounded a corner in the trail, he spotted a grassy area where some men had gathered. She could tell by their garments hat they were from Judea. She was certain that she had found the ones she was looking for.)ne of them especially caught her attention. He looked so calm and kind. *That must be Jesus, he Healer!* She ran toward Him, shouting, "Lord, have mercy on me! My daughter is severely ossessed of a demon!" (Matthew 15:22).

The gospel of Matthew tells the rest of the story:

> But [Jesus] answered her not a word. And His disciples came and urged Him, saying, "Send her away, for she cries out after us." But He answered and said, "I was not sent except to the lost sheep of the house of Israel." Then she came and worshiped Him, saying, "Lord, help me!" But He answered and said, "It is not good to take the children's bread and throw it to the little dogs." And she said, "Yes, Lord, yet even the little dogs eat the crumbs which fall from their masters' table." Then Jesus answered and said to her, "O woman, great is your faith! Let it be to you as you desire." And her daughter was healed from that very hour.

Elissa recognized in Jesus something far greater than in all the priests and rabbis she had met. She fell at His feet, not just to ask Him for help, but to *worship!* Elissa's search was over! She had not only found someone who could heal her daughter, but also someone who could fill her empty heart.

Many are mystified by this story, wondering why Jesus seemed to act in such an indifferent manner at first. He obviously didn't hold animosity toward this woman. Indeed,

He had already healed a Roman centurion's son, and spoke with a Samaritan woman, demonstrating to His followers that God's love, grace, and healing power were available to *everyone.* All along, Jesus had sought to break down the barriers between people—whether of race, religion, or gender.

On this day, it seems that Jesus was presenting a test to His disciples, determining if they had learned the lesson yet. Wouldn't it have been wonderful if, instead of trying to send her away, the disciples had urged Jesus, saying, "Lord, don't turn her away! This woman needs You!" I think that is what Jesus would have hoped for! But, as usual, the disciples were slow to learn. When Jesus enthusiastically commended Elissa for her faith and pronounced her child healed, they must have realized that they had failed the test. Jesus loved this woman; He was even amazed by her faith!

One of the most impressive things about this woman is how she did not allow the disciples' prejudice, or even Jesus' initial comments, to daunt her. She could have let pride fill her heart. She could have been offended and turned back. She could have turned inward with her pain and returned home to live out her days in isolation. But she didn't. She remained unafraid, ignoring the seeming indifference, staying focused on her mission and stepping forward in faith.

Are you willing to do the same?

The names Elissa and Chara have been added to help readers better differentiate the characters, who aren't named in the Scripture.

Conversation

"Without faith it is impossible to please Him, for he who comes to God must believe that He is, and that He is a rewarder of those who diligently seek Him" (Hebrews 11:6).

"By grace you have been saved through faith, and that not of yourselves; it is the gift of God" (Ephesians 2:8).

"Fight the good fight of faith, lay hold on eternal life, to which you were also called" (1 Timothy 6:12).

Daily Reflection

Lessons I Learned:

___

___

___

___

(Reflect on opportunities for self-improvement.)

Personal Goal for Today:

___

___

___

(Identify one goal based on the reading.)

Today's Targets:

1. ___
2. ___
3. ___

(List three practical steps to help you reach your goal.)

Today I am thankful for:

___

___

___

___

(Write a short prayer of thanks to God for the blessings He has brought to you.)

Day 26

Delivered from Demons

Colleen Townsley

> *"All that the Father gives Me will come to Me, and the one who comes to Me I will by no means cast out."* —John 6:37

Have you ever thought there is no hope for you–that you are too far gone to be saved?

She came to her senses, looked around at the people staring at her, and began to panic. *Where am I? What have I done this time? Why are they mocking me?* Fearing for her safety—but also feeling worthless and broken—she began to cry as she ran from the crowd in shame. Unfortunately, it wasn't fast enough. She heard the taunts and cruel comments. "Witch! She's drunk! Cursed of God! She should have gone to the synagogue like a good Jewish girl. Even a swine herder wouldn't want her!"

She made her way home and barricaded herself in her room, crying out to the Lord: "God, what is happening to me? Please stop the voices—I don't want to kill myself! I want You to love me. Please save me. I can't live this way anymore!" She sat there miserable, wondering if she really was cursed of God. She looked back on her life with regret and remorse. She realized how each poor choice led her down this path of destruction, but she couldn't see how to change her course. She fought through paranoia, pain, and voices—those incessant voices of doom and self-harm—to offer one last plea to the God of the universe: *Father, I've tried to save myself and failed every time. You alone can save me. Lord, only deliver me from this bondage and I will be Your devoted servant.*

The Bible doesn't tell us how the healing came about, only that Jesus healed her. "Now when he rose early on the first day of the week, He appeared first to Mary Magdalene, out of whom He had cast seven demons" (Mark 16:9). The Bible mentions "certain women who had been healed of evil spirits and infirmities—Mary called lagdalene, out of whom had come seven demons" (Luke 8:2). These days, it's easy to rush off demon possession as Old World hysteria or the ignorance of a bygone age; owever, the Bible is clear that sin is bondage. Bondage to Satan. Bondage is another vord for slavery. Slaves are possessions of their owners. Sinners are consequently, in a eal sense, possessed by Satan.

Some have speculated that the demons Mary was released from were pride, envy, nger, intemperance, lasciviousness, covetousness, and spiritual complacency. If that were rue, how many of us would be considered demon possessed? Such a sobering thought—et we need not despair.

> The Savior never passed by one soul, however sunken in sin, who was willing to receive the precious truths of heaven. To publicans and harlots his words were the beginning of a new life. Mary Magdalene, out of whom He cast seven devils, was the last at the Savior's tomb and the first whom He greeted in the morning of His resurrection. . . . Beneath an appearance of hatred and contempt, even beneath crime and degradation, may be hidden a soul that the grace of Christ will rescue to shine as a jewel in the Redeemer's crown (*Thoughts from the Mount of Blessing*, p. 129, 130).

There is always hope in Jesus. Mary, after having been healed by Him, realized this ruth and it changed her eternal destiny. Once freed from the shackles of sin, she began a fe of service to her Lord. Her sincere concern and care for Jesus before, during, and after lis crucifixion was a beautiful manifestation of the lessons she had learned as His disciple. she expressed deep gratitude for her liberation from the power of sin by serving Jesus in umility and faith. She was completely healed and, thus, completely surrendered her will nd her life to Him. She became a true servant of the Lord, understanding that Christ was he example she was to follow.

What an illustration for us today! There was nothing she could have done to save nerself. Her healing was a gift from God; her only part in it was acceptance. When she had finally come to the end of her rope and received the cleansing and subsequent healing from Christ, she served Him—not from a place of obligation or fear but from one of love and gratitude. She listened to the Teacher speak and willingly incorporated His teachings nto her life. Through daily contact with Christ, she gained strength and shunned fear. This owly woman succeeded where even the apostles failed.

Eaton S. Barrett writes of Mary Magdalene in the poem *Woman*:

> Not she with trait'rous kiss her Saviour stung,
> Not she denied Him with unholy tongue;
> She, while apostles shrank, could danger brave,
> Last at His cross, and earliest at His grave.

It is not hard to imagine the impact her transformation must have had on the people around her. Thinking about the crowds who had seen her in her deranged state, imagine their reaction when she returned to society a rational, peaceful, compassionate, loving, generous, godly woman. Mary, this lost soul possessed by seven demons, never betrayed her Lord, never hid her connection to Him, never wavered in her faith and, even through the despair of His death, was concerned only with serving Him. Her testimony is written in the Bible as a memorial of her faith. What an affirmation she received, being the first to see the risen Savior! We, too, can have such affirmation. We, too, need only accept the mercy, grace, cleansing, and healing from Christ and, in gratitude, share the same with others.

Would you like to accept God's healing mercy today?

"Then your light shall break forth like the morning, your healing shall spring forth speedily, and your righteousness shall go before you; the glory of the Lord shall be your rear guard" (Isaiah 58:8).

"In Him we have redemption through His blood, the forgiveness of sins, according to the riches of His grace" (Ephesians 1:7).

"The Spirit of the Lord is upon Me, because He has anointed Me to preach the gospel to the poor; He has sent Me to heal the brokenhearted, to proclaim liberty to the captives and recovery of sight to the blind, to set at liberty those who are oppressed" (Luke 4:18).

Lessons I Learned:

(Reflect on opportunities for self-improvement.)

Personal Goal for Today:

(Identify one goal based on the reading.)

Today's Targets:

1.
2.
3.

(List three practical steps to help you reach your goal.)

Today I am thankful for:

(Write a short prayer of thanks to God for the blessings He has brought to you.)

Day 27

Martha's Faith

Rosemary McKenzie

"I know your works, love, service, faith, and your patience; and as for your works, the last are more than the first."—Revelation 2:19

Are you looking for a balance in your life between service and faith?

Milan, Italy, is home to the world's only certified seven-star hotel. While Dubai's Al Arab claims to be a seven-star hotel, Alessandro Rosso, the owner of the TownHouse Galleria Milano, has done the work to earn the certification. Guests at the hotel are welcomed with extraordinary hospitality. They are paired with a personal butler who speaks their native language, provides customized meals, maintains strict confidentiality, and works to ensure tha their stay is memorable and relaxing.

Hospitality was Martha's gift! Jesus enjoyed visiting her family home in Bethany, where He found understanding and friendship in a peaceful home. Scripture consistently mentions Martha serving those who came into her sphere of influence (Luke 10:38; John 12:2). Jesus did not condemn her service of love, but in answer to her request for His help, He pointed out her greatest need. "Martha, Martha, you are worried and troubled about many things. But one thing is needed, and Mary has chosen that good part, which will not be taken away from her" (Luke 10:41, 42).

Martha was a devoted follower of Jesus. She is one of the first recorded women to confess her faith in Jesus as the Christ (John 11:27). But in the anxiety and stress of this moment, she was more concerned about her work in providing for Jesus than in understanding the important lessons about eternal life that He wanted to share with her.

Jesus identified Martha's challenge as worry, and He offered the solution, the "one thing" that was needed—to sit at His feet and listen to His Word (Luke 10:39). Her great need was to experience abiding faith in Him. Jesus invited Martha, as He invites you and me today, to be till, to listen, to understand who He is (Psalm 46:10), and to be transformed and sanctified through His Word of truth (John 17:17).

Jesus said, "If you abide in Me, and My words abide in you, you will ask what you desire, and it shall be done for you. By this My Father is glorified, that you bear much fruit; so you will be My disciples" (John 15:7, 8). The Scripture links time spent in God's Word with bearing fruit, or carrying out a service for Him. The fruit of faith is loving service for God. This is the identifying mark of His true disciples.

Today, like Martha, we often face challenges in knowing how to prioritize the responsibilities we face as women, sisters, daughters, mothers, and wives. We are encouraged that "The cause of Christ needs careful, energetic workers. There is a wide field for the Marthas, with their zeal in active religious work. But let them first sit with Mary at the feet of Jesus. Let diligence, promptness, and energy be sanctified by the grace of Christ; then the life will be an unconquerable power for good" (*The Desire of Ages*, p. 525).

We are invited to choose the good part, the part of transforming faith in Christ that is found by taking time in His Word. "So then faith comes by hearing, and hearing by the word of God" (Romans 10:17). As we abide in Christ and allow His Word to transform our lives, our faith is revealed in our service. James asks, "Do you see that faith was working together with his works, and by works faith was made perfect?" (James 2:22). The challenge of faith is allowing God to change us, our ideas, our priorities, our plans—to accomplish His greater plans in our lives.

In Revelation, God's end-time people are especially noted for two characteristics: "Here is the patience of the saints; here are those who keep the commandments of God and the faith of Jesus" (Revelation 14:12). The patience, perseverance, or steadfastness of God's people is demonstrated as their lives reflect the life of Jesus in their actions and words.

The Apostle John wrote, "Now by this we know that we know Him, if we keep His commandments. . . . whoever keeps His word, truly the love of God is perfected in him. By this we know that we are in Him. He who says he abides in Him ought himself also to walk just as He walked" (1 John 2:3, 5, 6).

Today, God needs women like Martha, women with energy, wisdom, and most of all faith. You and I have the opportunity to be these women, women who find their strength and inspiration in time spent with Jesus—learning of Him and gaining His wisdom and grace. Those who do this will be a power for good that cannot be measured. "A woman who fears the LORD, she shall be praised. . . . And let her own works praise her in the gates" (Proverbs 31:30, 31).

Would you like to be described this way? Would you like to be known as a woman of faith and service? In a world full of distractions and temptations, we are encouraged to stand strong in our faith. "Stand therefore, having girded your waist with truth, having put on the breastplate of righteousness, and having shod your feet with the preparation of the gospel of peace; above all, taking the shield of faith with which you will be able to quench all the fiery darts of the wicked one" (Ephesians 6:14–16).

You have the opportunity, today, to make the difference—to sit at Jesus' feet, to surrender your plans to His leading and follow the path of service that He lays out for you. As you demonstrate your faith in Him, you will see Him work for you in amazing ways. Today, Jesus is praying for you, as He prayed for His first disciples, that your faith will endure the trials ahead (Luke 22:32).

"Watch, stand fast in the faith, be brave, be strong" (1 Corinthians 16:13).

"As you therefore have received Christ Jesus the Lord, so walk in Him, rooted and built up in Him and established in the faith, as you have been taught, abounding in it with thanksgiving" (Colossians 2:6, 7).

"Fight the good fight of faith, lay hold on eternal life, to which you were also called and have confessed the good confession in the presence of many witnesses" (1 Timothy 6:12).

Lessons I Learned:

(Reflect on opportunities for self-improvement.)

Personal Goal for Today:

(Identify one goal based on the reading.)

Today's Targets:

1.
2.
3.

(List three practical steps to help you reach your goal.)

Today I am thankful for:

(Write a short prayer of thanks to God for the blessings He has brought to you.)

The Widow with Two Mites

Abby Osinjolu

"The generous soul will be made rich, and he who waters will also be watered himself." —Proverbs 11:25

Have you given your all to someone you love but felt like it was hardly noticed?

The court was busy as the people placed their offerings in the treasure chest. Many looked in awe and admiration as the rich poured out their large amounts with great display.

The widow may have thought sorrowfully, *How can I even compare?* The poor woman had only two mites, which was just enough to take care of her immediate needs. *Wouldn't it be better to wait until I can afford to give more?* After all, she wasn't guaranteed her next meal—and if she made this decision, she would be even more helpless than she was before. Perhaps she wondered if it would even be appreciated? After moments of consideration, she made her decision.

Hesitating, as though fearful of being seen, she approached the chest. As the rich paraded by to display their large offerings, she hovered in the background. The last thing she wanted was to be conspicuous. After waiting for an opportunity, though, she made her move, quickly threw in her two tiny mites, and turned to escape. But at that moment a voice arrested her attention. It was a voice like no other—melodious yet filled with power. "Truly I say to you that this poor widow has put in more than all; for all these out of their abundance have put in offerings for God, but she out of her poverty put in all the livelihood that she had" (Luke 21:3,4). How surprised and encouraged she must have felt to hear those beautiful words from Jesus!

God often works in ways that seem unusual and unappealing. By outward appearance, David was a young and weak shepherd boy, but God used him to deliver the children of Israel from their enemies. By outward appearance, Esther was an orphan with no promise of a future, but God granted her favor and set her as the king's wife, using her to free His people from persecution. By outward appearance, Jesus came as a babe to a poor family; as a man, He had no outward beauty that drew people to Him—and yet He was the Son of God.

God looks at the heart. He sees each desire to honor Him, and however small our gift may be, He gladly accepts it because it comes from a heart of love. So we can be glad knowing that our seemingly insignificant gifts are noticed by God.

> Not the great things which every eye sees and every tongue praises does God account most precious. The little duties cheerfully done, the little gifts which make no show, and which to human eyes may appear worthless, often stand highest in His sight. A heart of faith and love is dearer to God than the most costly gift (*Counsels on Stewardship*, p. 175, 176).

"What is in your hand?" my gardening teacher asked the class. *Nothing*, I thought, confused, as I took a quick glance. "What is in your hand?" he asked persistently. "What do you have? What can you give? What talents has God blessed you with? We all have something." Some students didn't believe they had any, but I began to think of the gifts I had. When you are at a loss as to what to do for God, always think about what is in your hand. This simple lesson has always stuck with me.

So what is in your hand today? What talents and spiritual gifts has God given you? Is it only two mites? Can you give only a smile? Then smile to best of your ability, and God will bless someone through you. Are you a good listener? Then listen intently and pray as people open the desires of their hearts to you. But I'm sure you have more talents than that. Did you know that time is a talent? And health? We could all do better in those areas. Do you know that you are making an impact on somebody's life without even realizing it? Do you have siblings, parents, friends, co-workers? If so, then you have the talent of influence. Why not use it, along with the talent of speech, to honor God?

Did you know that love is a talent? Actually, true love is a spiritual gift, which, according to the Bible, is the most important gift—one that we all need.

> Though I speak with the tongues of men and of angels, but have not love, I have become sounding brass or a clanging cymbal. And though I have the gift of prophecy, and understand all mysteries and all knowledge, and though I have all faith, so that I could remove mountains, but have not love, I am nothing (1 Corinthians 13:1, 2).

There are two kinds of love—worldly love and heavenly love. Worldly love only loves a few and can fade when it isn't returned or is severely tested. But heavenly love is precious and beautiful. It loves everyone and treats all with respect and dignity—even when it is treated with hate and scorn in return. That love, only Jesus can put into our hearts.

God has blessed you with so many talents. Will you surrender them to Him today? Do what you can. Like the poor widow, cast your two mites into the service of God. To the world your gift may seem insignificant, but to Christ, when given with a heart of love, it is of inestimable worth.

Conversation

"He who sows sparingly will also reap sparingly, and he who sows bountifully will also reap bountifully" (2 Corinthians 9:6).

"Let each one give as he purposes in his heart, not grudgingly or of necessity; for God loves a cheerful giver" (2 Corinthians 9:7).

"Give, and it will be given to you: good measure, pressed down, shaken together, and running over will be put into your bosom. For with the same measure that you use, it will be measured back to you" (Luke 6:38).

Lessons I Learned:

(Reflect on opportunities for self-improvement.)

Personal Goal for Today:

(Identify one goal based on the reading.)

Today's Targets:

1.
2.
3.

(List three practical steps to help you reach your goal.)

Today I am thankful for:

(Write a short prayer of thanks to God for the blessings He has brought to you.)

Day 29

Blessed by Giving

Pam Lascoe

"Do not forget to do good and to share, for with such sacrifices God is well pleased." —Hebrews 13:16

Who do you look to first for acceptance, approval, and love?

At one time or another throughout life, each of us makes sacrifices. These sacrifices come in many shapes and sizes, often changing in their worth and intention over the years. Some people are just generous. Some people are simply "doers" and, during the course of their lives, share their love and joy through giving by just doing without thinking twice—sometimes to the detriment of family and self.

When Christians offer sacrificial gifts, sometimes it is with a happy and generous heart, but sometimes it isn't. When we sacrifice to give with a grateful, loving heart—whether monetarily or through deed—that is the most valuable gift in the Lord's eyes.

Christ's example of great sacrifice shows how we are to give of ourselves. "Being found in appearance as a man, He humbled Himself and became obedient to the point of death, even the death of the cross" (Philippians 2:8). We are to give *all* we have.

As wives and mothers, sisters, daughters, and friends, women tend to sacrifice continually for family, friends, and others—because that is just what we do. Some certainly give more than others, but I don't know of any woman in my personal scope of influence that doesn't sacrifice for her family and those dear to the heart. We often give of ourselves in order to ensure the safety, well-being, and joy of those around us.

I don't know about you, but my personal life struggle is that I have always found it difficult to say "No" in almost any circumstance. Whether it was the teacher at school who needed supplies for a special event, or maybe one child forgot that project that just had to be finished "tomorrow," or that smelly soccer uniform that needed to be washed at midnight for an early morning wake-up call—mom was sure to help far into the wee hours to accomplish the task. And I could never say "no" to work-related tasks, events that required a little extra help. But these things sometimes got in the way of my husband and our marriage, and I realized that as givers, we need to be careful to strike a balance in our activities.

By far, my favorite thing is to share myself through creativity. Instead of speaking my feelings, I would prefer to create them in the form of gifts of food, cards, crocheted hats, scarves, or blankets, sharing my home, time, and resources with others—or anything to make a brother or sister feel better about themselves. The joy of doing and giving is indescribable. Unfortunately, there have been circumstances in my personal and physical life that have made it difficult to continue some of these gifts of sharing. These setbacks have often made me feel less competent and less capable as a woman, wife, and mother.

The story of Tabitha, or Dorcas, holds great promise for faithful "doers." Tabitha painstakingly provided women and widows in the community with desperately needed clothing. She was persistently giving to others. She was a doer. She was "full of good works and charitable deeds which she did" (Acts 9:36).

We know that one day she became ill and died, and all the women and saints in Joppa mourned her because she was such a wonderful, giving person. Indeed, she was so dearly loved that her friends couldn't give her up. "Since Lydda was near Joppa, and the disciples had heard that Peter was there, they sent two men to him, imploring him not to delay in coming to them" (verse 38). At their urgent request, the apostle Peter hurried to their town.

"When he had come, they brought him to the upper room. And all the widows stood by him weeping, showing the tunics and garments which Dorcas had made while she was with them. But Peter put them all out, and knelt down and prayed. And turning to the body he said, 'Tabitha, arise.' And she opened her eyes, and when she saw Peter she sat up" (verses 39, 40). He prayed and called Tabitha to rise—and she did! Through God's power and grace, her life was restored.

What can we learn from Tabitha? Perhaps that, by faith, our souls can be raised to life by opening our minds and hearts to the sacrifice given by our precious Lord. Maybe her life shows us that through true sacrificial giving, God can and will bless us and others we reach through a loving example of Christian service. It also shows us that we *must* look to God for love and acceptance first—not to others as we may often be inclined to do.

My innate insecurity makes me long for the acceptance and approval of others, so I won't say "No." But the lovely example of Tabitha, and so many others in the Bible, shows that I don't need the approval of others to be loved—or to be loving. "With goodwill doing service, as to the Lord, and not to men, knowing that whatever good anyone does, he will receive the same from the Lord" (Ephesians 6:7, 8).

The good that we do, we do to the Lord. With this revelation, I am now able to move forward and share—whether it's as simple as surprising a co-worker when she is feeling blue, sending a note of thanks and encouragement to a friend, telling my husband how much I appreciate all he does for the family, or simply sending a special care package to the child away at college. The little things I can do now are enough; after all, it's the little things we do and say that often make the biggest difference in the lives of others.

Just like Tabitha, we can bless so many people with a smile or a simple gesture of kindness, as long as we remember daily to see each person through the eyes of Jesus.

"Give, and it will be given to you: good measure, pressed down, shaken together, and running over will be put into your bosom. For with the same measure that you use, it will be measured back to you" (Luke 6:38).

"We are His workmanship, created in Christ Jesus for good works, which God prepared beforehand that we should walk in them" (Ephesians 2:10).

"Let us not grow weary while doing good, for in due season we shall reap if we do not lose heart" (Galatians 6:9).

Lessons I Learned:

(Reflect on opportunities for self-improvement.)

Personal Goal for Today:

(Identify one goal based on the reading.)

Today's Targets:

1. ___
2. ___
3. ___

(List three practical steps to help you reach your goal.)

Today I am thankful for:

(Write a short prayer of thanks to God for the blessings He has brought to you.)

Day 30

A Conversion of Immersion

Candice Scarpino

> *"When she and her household were baptized, she begged us, saying, 'If you have judged me to be faithful to the Lord, come to my house and stay.' So she persuaded us."* —Acts 16:15

Have you ever heard a teaching from the Bible that was so powerful it changed your life?

We don't know exactly what the apostle Paul taught at a river bank on a Sabbath day many, many years ago. But whatever he shared, it convicted a woman's heart and she *and* her household were baptized that same day. Who was this woman, and how may her brief but important story relate to Christian women today—especially those who desire to be baptized or re-baptized?

Who was Lydia? The Bible gives us a small glimpse into the who, what, where, when, and why. Her story is found in Acts 16:12–15:

> From there to Philippi, which is the foremost city of that part of Macedonia, a colony. And we were staying in that city for some days. And on the Sabbath day we went out of the city to the riverside, where prayer was customarily made; and we sat down and spoke to the women who met there. Now a certain woman named Lydia heard us. She was a seller of purple from the city of Thyatira, who worshiped God. The Lord opened her heart to heed the things spoken by Paul.

Two things stand out about this woman—she sold purple, and she was a woman who worshiped God. She also apparently kept the Sabbath. No doubt, Lydia worshiped the true God; that is, she changed her religion and become a converted believer to the Jewish faith. Paul, while living in Ephesus—south of the city of Philippi where Lydia now lived—had preached the good news. These teachings had spread widely since they were taught by several disciples in the young, growing Christian church.

The feminine name, Lydia, is a namesake for the region of Lydia in Asia Minor, which now constitutes several provinces in the country of Turkey. Perhaps Lydia's parents named her after their beloved homeland. In Greek and Persian translations, "Lydia" means "beautiful one" or "noble one."

Adam Clarke, in his *Bible Commentary*, states, "Lydian women have been celebrated for their beautiful purple manufactures." In Bible times, the color purple was most often worn by the rich or by nobility. To produce such elegant purple dyes for the affluent would have definitely been profitable for Lydia and other women in the trade. Specifically, she was a seller of purple from Thyatira—a prosperous city on the banks of the River Lycus, located in the Roman province of Asia—a place also well known as a trade center for indigo. It is also interesting to note that Lydia's home town of Thyatira is one of the named seven churches in Asia mentioned in Revelation 1:11. (See also Revelation 2:18–24.)

The Bible seems to indicate that it was her usual custom to meet with the other women at the river for prayer. And on one particular Sabbath day, Lydia was cut to the heart when Paul spoke to the group of women and shared the gospel with them.

Lydia was already a believer, at least to some extent. She worshiped the Creator, the God of heaven and earth. She no longer followed the teachings and practices of the ancient sun-god Tyrimnos or the goddess associated with him, Boreatene. No, she was a true-God worshiper—and yet her life was dramatically changed when the Lord opened her heart through Paul's words. "Lydia received the truth gladly. She and her household were converted and baptized, and she entreated the apostles to make her house their home" (*The Acts of the Apostles*, p. 212).

Lydia went from having some knowledge of God—and worshiping Him to the best of her ability—to receiving further enlightenment from the Holy Spirit and then dedicating herself and her family in a public baptism, including full-water immersion. What a testimony to her fellow Greek citizens!

She then became hospitable to the point of persuading the apostles to stay with her. This showed her deep gratitude for their sharing of truth with her. What a blessing it must have been to have the apostles as her guests. One can just imagine Lydia inviting friends and other family members to her home to hear more about Jesus and perhaps be baptized.

Maybe you are a Christian who has always wanted to become baptized. Or maybe you have been baptized for years but have never heard the truth of Jesus' soon return and the *manner* of His return. Perhaps you've never heard it taught that when people die they are actually "sleeping in Jesus" until Resurrection Day. Many times, those convicted by the Holy Spirit live up to the truth they know but have an incomplete picture. But God continues working in our lives to bring us to a fuller understanding of His truth. "You shall know the truth, and the truth shall make you free" (John 8:32). There are still many "Lydias" out there who may experience a conversion of immersion like never before!

Conversation

"You will light my lamp; the Lord my God will enlighten my darkness" (Psalm 18:28).

"The statutes of the Lord are right, rejoicing the heart; the commandment of the Lord is pure, enlightening the eyes; the fear of the Lord is clean, enduring forever; the judgments of the Lord are true and righteous altogether" (Psalm 19:8, 9).

"That their hearts may be encouraged, being knit together in love, and attaining to all riches of the full assurance of understanding, to the knowledge of the mystery of God, both of the Father and of Christ, in whom are hidden all the treasures of wisdom and knowledge" (Colossians 2:2, 3).

Daily Reflection

Lessons I Learned:

(Reflect on opportunities for self-improvement.)

Personal Goal for Today:

(Identify one goal based on the reading.)

Today's Targets:

1.
2.
3.

(List three practical steps to help you reach your goal.)

Today I am thankful for:

(Write a short prayer of thanks to God for the blessings He has brought to you.)

Day 31

A Willing Heart

Cari Anderson

"Well done, good and faithful servant; you have been faithful over a few things, I will make you ruler over many things. Enter into the joy of your Lord." —Matthew 25:23

Have you ever felt you were not qualified to do the Lord's work or that your efforts to witness didn't make a difference to others?

A missionary in Africa once met an elderly woman who had learned about the gospel truth. She was also blind, unable to read or write, but she was so excited about her new faith that she wanted to share it with others.

One day, she went to the missionary and asked if he could obtain a French-language Bible for her. After she had received the Bible, she once again went to the missionary and asked, "Will you please highlight John 3:16 in red and mark the page so I can find it?" He did as she asked.

Intrigued, the missionary accompanied her the next day to see what she would do. In the afternoon, she made her way up to the local school's front door as the children were being dismissed. When she heard kids coming out, she stopped each one to ask, "Can you read French?"

When one of them would say "Yes," she then asked him to read the red highlighted passage from the page marked in her Bible. After he read the passage aloud to her, she asked, "Do you know what this means?" She would then tell him all about Jesus.

The missionary later confirmed that, as a result of her faithful efforts over the years, twenty-four boys from the school became pastors.[7]

Just like this faithful elderly woman, Priscilla, along with her husband Aquila, led souls like Apollos to Christ—armed only with the abilities and knowledge that God gave her. Who was Priscilla?

The first time we read about her is in Acts 18:1, 2:

> After these things Paul departed from Athens and went to Corinth. And He found a certain Jew named Aquila, born in Pontus, who had recently come from Italy with his wife Priscilla ... and he came to them.

Like the apostle Paul, Priscilla and her husband were tent makers. They graciously invited Paul to stay with them as they worked together in making tents and teaching the Word of God to the locals.

Making tents wasn't the most glamorous job, but Priscilla was willing to assist in the work—likely because it enabled Paul and her husband to support themselves as they continued in the Lord's work. (See Proverbs 31:13.)

Priscilla and her husband also served as foreign missionaries, sailing with Paul to Syria and later to Ephesus, where Paul left them to continue the work. Not long after, as documented in Acts 18:24, the two met Apollos, "an eloquent man and mighty in the Scriptures." While God had been using Apollos in a mighty way even on the incomplete knowledge he had, Priscilla and her husband recognized immediately an opportunity to witness to him. They taught him the "way of God more accurately" and, because of their mentoring, Apollos became a powerful evangelist for Christ among the Jews.

Although Priscilla was a "mere" tent maker, God still worked through her as she humbled herself, willing to be a faithful servant in all God called her to do. Beyond working for God in personal ministry, Priscilla was even willing to risk her life for the cause of Christ. (See Romans 16:3, 4.) Jesus said, "Greater love has no one than this, than to lay down one's life for his friends" (John 15:13).

You may have been asking yourself, *How can God use an ordinary person like me? How can I make a difference?*—after all, I'm only one person. Maybe you think you don't have sufficient knowledge of the Bible to teach others. Perhaps you don't feel qualified to do God's work at all.

Be of good courage! The blind elderly woman could easily have thought she was not qualified to work for God. Yet, despite her disability, she faithfully did her part and God blessed her in her work and gave her victories for His kingdom. The same was true for Priscilla. She could have easily thought that she lacked the qualifications to do the Lord's work. Yet she resolved to serve God faithfully in whatever He called her to do. The results were so spectacular that God inspired Paul to write about her so we could read her story some two thousand years later!

Likewise, if you embrace the same dedication and love toward the Lord as Priscilla, you'll have stories to tell in the eternity to come. God can and will use you to share with others His love if you are willing. It might be as simple as being a friend to someone who, like Apollos, will one day become a mighty soul winner for the Lord. You might plant a seed that the Lord can use when you invite someone into your home to tell them about God.

You can have the assurance that when you work for God, faithfully using whatever abilities He has granted, you will be part of enlarging His kingdom. Jesus said, in John 16:13, "When He, the Spirit of truth, has come, He will guide you into all truth; for He will not speak on His own authority, but whatever He hears He will speak; and He will tell you things to come." Isn't that a wonderful promise? As we serve Jesus from day to day, even in our limitations, we know that we won't be alone. He has already given us the Holy Spirit to guide us into all truth and to help us as we witness to others of Jesus' love.

Are you willing, today, to use the gifts God has given you? In doing so, you can be a faithful witness to others.

Conversation

"Whatever you do in word or deed, do all in the name of the Lord Jesus, giving thanks to God the Father through Him" (Colossians 3:17).

"God is not unjust to forget your work and labor of love which you have shown toward His name, in that you have ministered to the saints, and do minister" (Hebrews 6:10).

"My beloved brethren, be steadfast, immovable, always abounding in the work of the Lord, knowing that your labor is not in vain in the Lord" (1 Corinthians 15:58).

---

7 Adapted from *Colossians and Philemon: The Supremacy of Christ* by R. Kent Hughes, as seen at http://ministry127.com/resources/illustration/a-blind-illiterate-soulwinner

Lessons I Learned:

(Reflect on opportunities for self-improvement.)

Personal Goal for Today:

(Identify one goal based on the reading.)

Today's Targets:

1.
2.
3.

(List three practical steps to help you reach your goal.)

Today I am thankful for:

(Write a short prayer of thanks to God for the blessings He has brought to you.)